Catholic Astronomy: The Vatican Observatory's Pioneering Contributions

Larry Culver

Published by Larry Culver, 2024.

While every precaution has been taken in the preparation of this book, the publisher assumes no responsibility for errors or omissions, or for damages resulting from the use of the information contained herein.

CATHOLIC ASTRONOMY: THE VATICAN OBSERVATORY'S PIONEERING CONTRIBUTIONS

First edition. February 12, 2024.

Written by Larry Culver.

Preface

Explore the complete history of the Vatican Observatory and the people behind its scientific endeavors. This book aims to educate readers on the Vatican's enduring contributions to astronomy and its dialogue with cosmology and physics. The narrative emotionally amplifies the connection to the Catholic Church's real-world ideals, allowing readers to witness God's actions in the pursuit of understanding the cosmos and the daily events that shape our lives.

This book delves into the rich history of the Vatican Observatory, offering readers a comprehensive understanding of its origins, key figures, challenges, and its unique relationship with the Catholic Church. The book begins with an exploration of the founding of the Vatican Observatory, tracing its establishment back to its origins in 1580 under the patronage of Pope Gregory XIII. It highlights the significance of this institution as one of the oldest astronomical observatories globally. Subsequently, the narrative delves into the early pioneers of the Vatican Observatory, showcasing the contributions of notable figures who played pivotal roles in advancing astronomical research within the Catholic Church. The book then navigates through the challenges faced by the observatory throughout its history. Finally, the book examines the Vatican Observatory's relationship with the Catholic Church, emphasizing its alignment with the Church's broader mission and its role in fostering dialogue between science and theology. Through a nuanced exploration of these topics, the stage is set for a deeper exploration of the Vatican Observatory's enduring legacy in the subsequent chapters of the book.

Table Of Contents

Chapter 1: The Vatican Observatory - A Brief History

"Unveiling the Celestial Nexus: Exploring the Nexus of Science and Faith Through the Vatican Observatory's Illustrious History"

The Founding of the Vatican Observatory

The Vatican Observatory stands as a testament to the profound connection between science and religion. Its establishment marked a significant chapter in the history of astronomy, and its pioneering contributions have greatly influenced the field. This subchapter delves into the origins and early days of the Vatican Observatory, shedding light on its mission and the impact it has had on both astronomy and Catholicism.

The roots of the Vatican Observatory can be traced back to the late 16th century when Pope Gregory XIII commissioned the Gregorian calendar reform. Pope Gregory XIII, born Ugo Boncompagni on January 7, 1502, served as the head of the Catholic Church from May 13, 1572, until his death on April 10, 1585. One of the most notable achievements during his papacy was the implementation of the Gregorian calendar, a reform that aimed to correct inaccuracies in the Julian calendar and bring the date of the spring equinox closer to March 21. This adjustment addressed issues with the timing of the celebration of Easter and improved the accuracy of the calendar in alignment with astronomical phenomena.

Pope Gregory XIII's papacy was marked by efforts to strengthen the Catholic Church in the face of the Protestant Reformation. He actively supported the Jesuit order and sought to combat the spread of Protestantism. His leadership played a crucial role in organizing the Council of Trent, which addressed doctrinal and disciplinary issues within the Catholic Church and contributed to the Counter-Reformation.

In addition to his contributions to the Church, Pope Gregory XIII was a patron of the arts and sciences. He supported the construction of the Gregorian Tower, an astronomical observatory, as part of the Vatican Observatory. His interest in astronomy was not only theological but also practical, as demonstrated by his commissioning of the Gregorian calendar.

The Gregorian calendar, introduced in October 1582, was a significant reform that realigned the calendar year with the solar year. It addressed the discrepancy between the calendar and the Earth's revolutions around the sun, bringing about a more accurate calculation of leap years. The adoption of the Gregorian calendar was not immediate worldwide but eventually became the standard calendar for much of the world, contributing to its enduring legacy.

Pope Gregory XIII's papacy left an indelible mark on both the Catholic Church and the world at large. The Gregorian calendar remains in use today, attesting to the enduring impact of his efforts to reconcile the Church's liturgical calendar with the natural rhythms of the cosmos.

However, it was not until 1891, under the leadership of Pope Leo XIII, that the Vatican Observatory was officially founded. Pope Leo XIII recognized the need for the Catholic Church to engage with the scientific community and support scientific research. He appointed Father Angelo Secchi, a renowned astronomer, as the first director of the Vatican Observatory.

Pope Leo XIII, born Vincenzo Gioacchino Raffaele Luigi Pecci on March 2, 1810, served as the head of the Catholic Church from February 20, 1878, until his death on July 20, 1903, making him one of the longest-reigning popes in history. His papacy was marked by a commitment to addressing the challenges posed by the rapidly changing political, social, and economic landscape of the late 19th century.

Leo XIII is often remembered for his landmark encyclical "Rerum Novarum," issued in 1891. This encyclical addressed the social and economic problems arising from the Industrial Revolution and laid the groundwork for the Catholic Church's social teachings. "Rerum Novarum" advocated for the rights of workers, the importance of social justice, and the need for a just distribution of wealth. It emphasized the dignity of labor and called for cooperation between labor and capital.

Another significant aspect of Pope Leo XIII's pontificate was his effort to reconcile the Catholic Church with modern thought and culture. He sought to engage with intellectual currents of the time, encouraging a dialogue between faith and reason. While affirming traditional teachings, Leo XIII recognized the importance of engaging with contemporary ideas and promoting education and scholarship within the Church.

Leo XIII also played a key role in diplomatic efforts, working to maintain the Church's presence on the international stage. He fostered relationships with various nations and engaged in diplomatic initiatives, contributing to the Church's efforts to navigate the complex political dynamics of the late 19th and early 20th centuries.

Pope Leo XIII's dedication to ecumenism was evident in his efforts to foster dialogue with other Christian denominations and even non-Christian religions. He promoted unity among Christians and sought common ground on issues of shared concern.

Leo XIII's papacy left a lasting impact on the Catholic Church, particularly through his social teachings and efforts to reconcile the Church with the challenges of the modern world. His commitment to addressing social injustices and promoting the Church's engagement with contemporary thought influenced subsequent popes and contributed to the ongoing development of Catholic social doctrine.

The Vatican Observatory's mission was twofold: to advance scientific knowledge in the field of astronomy and to bridge the gap between science and faith. Father Secchi dedicated himself to this mission and established the observatory as a center for cutting-edge research. Under his leadership, the Vatican Observatory made significant contributions to the study of solar physics, stellar spectroscopy, and the mapping of the night sky.

Over the years, the Vatican Observatory has continued to play a crucial role in advancing our understanding of the universe. It has attracted talented astronomers from around the world, fostering an environment of collaboration and innovation. The observatory's research has led to groundbreaking discoveries, such as the confirmation of the Big Bang theory and the identification of exoplanets.

The Vatican Observatory's contributions to astronomy have not only expanded our knowledge of the cosmos but also strengthened the relationship between science and Catholicism. By embracing scientific inquiry, the Catholic Church has shown that faith and reason can coexist harmoniously. The Vatican Observatory serves as a symbol of this harmonious integration, inspiring both amateur astronomers and Catholics alike.

The founding of the Vatican Observatory marked a pivotal moment in the history of astronomy. Its commitment to scientific research and its efforts to bridge the gap between science and faith have positioned it as a leading institution in the field. The contributions of the Vatican Observatory have enriched our understanding of the universe while demonstrating the compatibility of science and Catholicism.

Early Pioneers of the Vatican Observatory

The Vatican Observatory has a rich and storied history, with a legacy of pioneering contributions to the field of astronomy. Over the years, several brilliant minds have dedicated their lives to furthering our understanding of the cosmos, all under the auspices of the Catholic Church. In this subchapter, we will explore the early pioneers of the Vatican Observatory and their invaluable contributions.

Father Christoph Clavius was a Jesuit mathematician from the Roman College, who was involved in the reform of the calendar and played a significant role in the early stages of the Observatory.

Father Angelo Secchi (1818–1878) was an Italian Jesuit priest, astronomer, and pioneer in astrophysics. Born in Reggio Emilia, Italy, Secchi joined the Jesuit order and became a prominent figure in 19th-century astronomy. His contributions spanned various areas, including solar physics, stellar spectroscopy, and the study of the planets. Father Secchi was appointed as the director of the observatory in 1865 and quickly made significant advancements in the field of spectroscopy. He developed a system of categorizing stars based on their spectral characteristics, known as the Secchi classification, which is still widely used today. His work laid the foundation for our understanding of stellar composition and greatly influenced the field of astrophysics.

Secchi's work in solar physics was groundbreaking. He made significant contributions to the understanding of the Sun's structure and activity. Using a spectroscope, he analyzed the solar spectrum and identified distinct absorption lines, classifying sunspots into four types based on their spectral characteristics. This classification system, known as the Secchi classes, became widely adopted in solar astronomy.

In addition to his solar research, Secchi made pioneering contributions to stellar astronomy. He was one of the first astronomers to systematically classify stars based on their spectra, laying the foundation for modern stellar spectroscopy. His work in this area led to the identification of different stellar types and provided valuable insights into the composition and evolution of stars.

Father Angelo Secchi's legacy extends beyond his scientific contributions. He was a dedicated educator and popularizer of science, striving to make astronomical knowledge accessible to a broader audience. His efforts included public lectures, writing, and the use of innovative teaching methods. Secchi's impact on both the scientific community and the public helped shape the field of astrophysics and contributed to the popularization of astronomy in the 19th century.

Another influential pioneer of the Vatican Observatory was Father Georges Lemaître, a Belgian Catholic priest and physicist. Father Georges Lemaître (1894–1966) was also a mathematician and astronomer who made groundbreaking contributions to the field of cosmology. Born in Charleroi, Belgium, Lemaître served as an artillery officer during World War I and was ordained as a Catholic priest in 1923 while also pursuing studies in mathematics and physics. His dual background in science and theology uniquely positioned him to engage in profound reflections on the nature of the universe. He studied at the University of Cambridge, the Massachusetts Institute of Technology (MIT), and the Harvard College Observatory, where he developed his interest in cosmology.

One of Father Lemaître's most significant contributions was the proposal of what is now known as the "Big Bang" theory. In 1927, Lemaître published a paper in which he suggested that the universe was expanding and could be traced back to an initial state of extremely high density. He theorized that the universe began as a "primeval atom," a term he coined, and then expanded over time. This concept laid the groundwork for the modern understanding of the origin of the universe and was a key development in cosmology. Despite the scientific merit of his idea, Lemaître faced initial skepticism, but his work gained recognition and acceptance as observational evidence supporting an expanding universe emerged. Father Georges Lemaître and Albert Einstein had limited direct interactions and communications regarding the "Big Bang Theory." However, Lemaître's work and ideas, which eventually led to the formulation of the Big Bang Theory, were influenced by Einstein's general

theory of relativity.

In addition to his contributions to cosmology, Father Georges Lemaître was an accomplished scientist and educator. He held various academic positions and served as a professor at the Catholic University of Leuven. Lemaître was also a member of the Pontifical Academy of Sciences, where he engaged in a fruitful dialogue between science and religion, served as president from 1960 until his death in 1966, and was instrumental in the development of modern cosmology and contributed to the understanding of cosmic rays and the three-body problem in physics. His humility and commitment to the pursuit of knowledge in both scientific and theological domains exemplify the compatibility of faith and reason.

Father Georges Lemaître's visionary ideas continue to shape our understanding of the universe's origins, and his legacy reflects the potential for harmony between science and faith, demonstrating that individuals can contribute meaningfully to both realms. His groundbreaking work paved the way for modern cosmology and earned him widespread recognition as one of the greatest scientific minds of the 20th century.

Lemaître's work was recognized with several awards, including the Francqui Prize in 1934 and the Eddington Medal in 1953. Despite his significant contributions to science, Lemaître maintained a strong commitment to his religious life, including daily private prayer and annual retreats. Lemaître's relationship with the Vatican was notable, especially with Pope Pius XII, who was interested in his work. Lemaître, however, cautioned against using his scientific theories as a validation of religious doctrine, emphasizing the separate realms of science and faith.

The Catholic Church's reaction to Georges Lemaître's Big Bang theory was notably positive, especially when compared to historical instances where scientific discoveries faced ecclesiastical opposition. Unlike Galileo's conflict with the Church or Johannes Kepler's excommunication by the Lutheran Church, Lemaître, a Roman Catholic priest and the proposer of the Big Bang theory, received support from the Vatican, particularly from Pope Pius XII.

Father Erwin Hubble, although not directly affiliated with the Vatican Observatory, also played a significant role in its early years. As a Catholic astronomer, Hubble made groundbreaking discoveries that supported the expanding universe theory, which complemented Father Lemaître's Big Bang theory. His observations of distant galaxies and their redshifts provided strong evidence for the expansion of the universe, confirming the revolutionary ideas put forth by Father Lemaître.

These early pioneers of the Vatican Observatory, along with many others, have left an indelible mark on the field of astronomy. Their dedication to scientific inquiry, coupled with their faith, allowed them to make groundbreaking discoveries that continue to shape our understanding of the cosmos. Their contributions serve as a testament to the compatibility of science and religion, highlighting the important role that the Catholic Church has played in advancing our knowledge of the universe.

For amateur astronomers and Catholics alike, the pioneering contributions of the Vatican Observatory are a source of inspiration and fascination. The early pioneers paved the way for future generations of astronomers to continue pushing the boundaries of our knowledge. By celebrating their achievements and studying their methodologies, we can gain a deeper appreciation for the intersection of faith and science and the profound impact it has had on our understanding of the universe.

Challenges Faced by the Vatican Observatory

The Vatican Observatory has a rich and storied history, marked by its pioneering contributions to the field of astronomy. However, like any scientific institution, it has faced its fair share of challenges along the way. This subchapter explores some of the obstacles that the Vatican Observatory has encountered and overcome, highlighting the dedication and perseverance of its astronomers.

One of the earliest challenges was the nationalization of the Observatory by the Italian government after the death of Father Angelo Secchi in 1878. This event effectively ended astronomical research in the Vatican until Pope Leo XIII re-founded the Specola Vaticana (Vatican Observatory) in 1891.

Another challenge faced by the Vatican Observatory is the delicate balance it must strike between science and religion. As an institution under the authority of the Catholic Church, the observatory has had to navigate the tensions that can arise between scientific inquiry and religious doctrine. This challenge has required astronomers at the Vatican Observatory to approach their research with a unique perspective, finding ways to reconcile the mysteries of the universe with their faith.

Another significant challenge that the Vatican Observatory has faced is the need to adapt to rapidly evolving technologies. From the early days of its establishment, the observatory has embraced cutting-edge instruments and techniques to advance its astronomical studies. However, this constant need to stay at the forefront of technological advancements has required significant resources and investments. Like any astronomical observatory, the Vatican Observatory has had to continually update and modernize its observational equipment. The need for advanced telescopes, detectors, and other instruments has posed financial and logistical challenges, requiring ongoing efforts to stay at the forefront of astronomical research.

Light pollution has been a significant challenge for the Vatican Observatory. Initially located within Vatican City, the Observatory was moved to Castel Gandolfo in the 1930s to escape the light pollution of Rome. However, the problem persisted, leading to the establishment of a second research center, the Vatican Observatory Research Group (VORG), in Tucson, Arizona, in 1981.

Financial constraints have also posed challenges for the Vatican Observatory. Like many scientific institutions, the Vatican Observatory has faced resource limitations, including financial constraints and staffing challenges. These limitations can impact the scope and scale of research projects, the maintenance of facilities, and the pursuit of cutting-edge advancements in astronomy. As a non-profit scientific institution, it relies on funding from both the Catholic Church and external sources. Securing funding for research projects, maintaining and upgrading equipment, and supporting its staff have all been ongoing challenges for the observatory. Nonetheless, the dedication and passion of its astronomers have allowed them to overcome these financial hurdles and continue their groundbreaking work.

The Vatican Observatory, operating at the intersection of science and religion, has at times faced public misconceptions. Clarifying its mission, objectives, and the nature of its scientific research has been essential in dispelling misunderstandings and promoting a more accurate understanding of the observatory's work. Throughout its history, it has had to navigate political and social climates that may not always be supportive of scientific pursuits. However, the observatory has remained steadfast in its commitment to advancing our understanding of the cosmos, even in the face of adversity. As an institution under the Holy See, the Vatican Observatory navigates the complex terrain of interdisciplinary dialogue between science and theology. Balancing perspectives from scientists and theologians and addressing questions related to the compatibility of scientific discoveries with religious beliefs has been an ongoing challenge.

Despite these challenges, the Vatican Observatory has made significant contributions to the field of astronomy. Its dedication to scientific inquiry and its ability to reconcile faith and reason have allowed it to overcome these obstacles. Today, the observatory stands as a testament to the power of collaboration between science and religion, inspiring amateur astronomers and Catholics alike with its pioneering contributions.

The Vatican Observatory's Relationship with the Catholic Church

The Vatican Observatory's relationship with the Catholic Church is a unique and fascinating one. Established in 1891 by Pope Leo XIII, the Vatican Observatory has made significant contributions to the field of astronomy while maintaining a strong connection to its Catholic roots. The Vatican Observatory has a unique relationship with the Catholic Church, as it is an astronomical research institution that operates under the authority of the Holy See. What makes the Vatican Observatory special is that it is part of the Vatican City State, which is the smallest independent city-state in the world and the spiritual and administrative headquarters of the Catholic Church. The observatory operates with the support of the Church and the Vatican, and its work aligns with the Church's broader commitment to the exploration of the natural world and the pursuit of knowledge.

At its core, the Vatican Observatory seeks to bridge the gap between faith and science, recognizing that both can coexist harmoniously. This approach is rooted in the belief that the study of the natural world can deepen our understanding and appreciation of God's creation. By exploring the mysteries of the universe, the Vatican Observatory strives to uncover the beauty and order that exist in the cosmos.

One of the key aspects of the observatory's relationship with the Catholic Church is its commitment to educating the faithful about the wonders of the universe. It has played a vital role in promoting the idea that science and religion are not mutually exclusive, but rather can complement and inform each other. Through lectures, publications, and other forms of outreach, the Vatican Observatory has sought to engage Catholics in a dialogue about the relationship between faith and reason.

The observatory's pioneering contributions to astronomy have been widely recognized and celebrated by both amateur astronomers and Catholics alike. In its early years, the Vatican Observatory made significant advancements in the study of comets, asteroids, and stellar parallax. Today, it continues to contribute to the field through its research on topics such as galactic dynamics, stellar evolution, and cosmology.

One of the most notable contributions of the Vatican Observatory is its participation in international collaborations and research projects. By working alongside astronomers from around the world, the observatory has fostered a spirit of cooperation and shared discovery. This collaborative approach reflects the Catholic Church's commitment to dialogue and engagement with the broader scientific community.

The Vatican Observatory's relationship with the Catholic Church is a testament to the harmonious coexistence of faith and science. By exploring the mysteries of the universe, the observatory seeks to deepen our understanding of God's creation and inspire awe and wonder. Its pioneering contributions to astronomy have made a significant impact on the field, earning recognition from both amateur astronomers and Catholics alike. By fostering dialogue and collaboration, the Vatican Observatory exemplifies the Catholic Church's commitment to engaging with science and promoting a holistic understanding of the world. In summary, the Vatican Observatory is a scientific institution that explores the mysteries of the universe, and its relationship with the Catholic Church reflects the Church's recognition of the value of scientific inquiry and the compatibility of faith and reason.

Chapter 2: The Vatican Observatory's Role in Advancing Astronomy

"The Vatican Observatory's Astronomical Odyssey in Advancing our Understanding of the Universe"

Contributions to Observational Astronomy

Observational astronomy, the study of celestial objects and phenomena through direct observation, has been a fundamental aspect of scientific exploration for centuries. In the realm of astronomy, the Vatican Observatory has played a pioneering role, making significant contributions that have shaped our understanding of the universe. This subchapter delves into the remarkable contributions of the Vatican Observatory to observational astronomy, highlighting its unique perspective as an institution rooted in both science and Catholicism.

From its establishment in 1891, the Vatican Observatory has been at the forefront of astronomical research. The observatory's early astronomers made groundbreaking observations, including the mapping of the lunar surface and the study of variable stars. Their meticulous recordings laid the foundation for future explorations in the field.

One notable contribution of the Vatican Observatory is its involvement in the study of asteroids. With the advent of powerful telescopes, astronomers at the observatory dedicated their efforts to cataloging and tracking these celestial objects. Their work not only identified numerous asteroids but also provided valuable data for understanding the formation and evolution of our solar system. Brother Guy Consolmagno, the observatory's director, has focused his research on asteroids and meteorites. His work has provided valuable insights into the physical properties of these celestial bodies, which are essential for understanding the early solar system and potential impact hazards.

Another area in which the Vatican Observatory has made significant contributions is the study of stellar spectra. By analyzing the light emitted by stars, astronomers can determine their composition, temperature, and other vital characteristics. The observatory's astronomers have made significant advancements in spectroscopy, contributing to our understanding of stellar evolution and the composition of distant galaxies.

The Vatican Observatory was involved in the creation of the Carte du Ciel, the first photographic survey of the entire sky. This project, conducted in collaboration with 19 other observatories around the world, produced a comprehensive map of the night sky, serving as a baseline for modern surveys.

The observatory's scientists have also conducted research in areas such as stellar evolution and galaxy clusters. This work has contributed to our understanding of the life cycles of stars and the formation and dynamics of galaxy clusters.

Moreover, the Vatican Observatory has actively participated in global collaborations and astronomical expeditions. Its astronomers have taken part in landmark projects such as the Hubble Space Telescope observations and the study of gamma-ray bursts. These collaborations have allowed the Vatican Observatory to contribute to cutting-edge research and expand our knowledge of the cosmos.

Beyond its scientific contributions, the Vatican Observatory also emphasizes the dialogue between science and faith. As an institution rooted in Catholicism, it actively promotes the compatibility of science and religion. By fostering this dialogue, the observatory encourages a holistic understanding of the universe that encompasses both scientific exploration and spiritual contemplation.

In conclusion, the Vatican Observatory's contributions to observational astronomy are both numerous and profound. Its astronomers have made significant strides in mapping the lunar surface, studying asteroids, analyzing stellar spectra, and engaging in global collaborations. Moreover, the observatory's unique perspective as a bridge between science and Catholicism enriches the scientific community and promotes a more holistic understanding of the universe. For amateur astronomers and Catholics alike, the Vatican

Observatory's pioneering contributions stand as a testament to the harmonious coexistence of faith and scientific exploration.

Early Observations and Discoveries

The subchapter "Early Observations and Discoveries" delves into the fascinating world of Catholic Astronomy, focusing on the pioneering contributions made by the Vatican Observatory. This section of the book is specifically designed for amateur astronomers, Catholics, and those interested in exploring the invaluable contributions of the Vatican Observatory to the field of astronomy.

The Vatican Observatory has a long and rich history, dating back to its establishment in 1891. From its inception, the observatory has been committed to advancing our understanding of the universe through scientific research and observation. This subchapter sheds light on the early observations and discoveries that laid the foundation for the Vatican Observatory's groundbreaking work.

One of the most notable early contributions of the observatory was the study of celestial objects, including stars, planets, and galaxies. The Vatican astronomers meticulously observed and recorded the positions, movements, and characteristics of these celestial bodies, contributing significantly to the development of astronomical knowledge.

Through these observations, the Vatican Observatory played a crucial role in the refinement of our understanding of the motion of planetary bodies. Their meticulous records and calculations helped to improve the accuracy of astronomical predictions, furthering our understanding of the laws governing the cosmos.

Another groundbreaking discovery made by the Vatican Observatory was its contribution to the study of comets. These celestial bodies, shrouded in mystery for centuries, were meticulously observed and studied by the Vatican astronomers. Their observations provided valuable insights into the nature and composition of comets, shedding light on their origins and behavior.

Furthermore, the Vatican Observatory's early observations and discoveries also included the study of nebulae and galaxies. By meticulously observing these distant cosmic objects, astronomers at the Vatican Observatory contributed significantly to our understanding of the structure and evolution of the universe.

This subchapter also highlights the significance of the Vatican Observatory's early contributions to the field of astrophysics. By analyzing the light emitted by stars and other celestial objects, Vatican astronomers were able to unravel the mysteries of stellar evolution and the physical processes occurring within stars. Father Angelo Secchi, a Jesuit priest and astronomer associated with the Vatican Observatory, was the first to use spectroscopy to classify stars into different types. This pioneering work laid the foundation for modern stellar classification and our understanding of the composition and properties of stars.

The "Early Observations and Discoveries" serves as a window into the pioneering contributions of the Vatican Observatory. It illuminates the crucial role played by the observatory in advancing our understanding of the universe through meticulous observation and scientific research. Whether you are an astronomy buff, a Catholic, or simply intrigued by the contributions of the Vatican Observatory to astronomy, this subchapter offers a captivating journey through the early discoveries and observations that laid the foundation for the groundbreaking work carried out by the Vatican astronomers.

Modern Observational Techniques

In recent years, advancements in technology have revolutionized the field of astronomy, allowing scientists to gain unprecedented insights into the workings of the universe. This subchapter explores the modern observational techniques that have been instrumental in the Vatican Observatory's pioneering contributions to the field of astronomy.

One of the most significant developments in modern observational techniques is the use of space-based telescopes. These cutting-edge instruments, such as the Hubble Space Telescope, have the advantage of being positioned above the Earth's atmosphere, which eliminates atmospheric distortion and provides incredibly sharp and detailed images of celestial objects. The Vatican Observatory has been actively involved in utilizing space-based telescopes to study various aspects of the universe, from distant galaxies to exoplanets.

Another breakthrough in observational techniques is the advent of radio astronomy. By detecting and analyzing radio waves emitted by celestial objects, astronomers can uncover hidden phenomena and gain insights into the universe's mysteries. The Vatican Observatory has been at the forefront of radio astronomy, collaborating with international partners to build and operate state-of-the-art radio telescopes. These telescopes have helped astronomers study cosmic microwave background radiation, map the distribution of galaxies, and search for signs of extraterrestrial life.

In addition to space-based telescopes and radio astronomy, the Vatican Observatory has embraced the use of advanced imaging technologies. Digital detectors, such as charge-coupled devices (CCDs), have replaced traditional photographic plates, allowing astronomers to capture and analyze light more efficiently. With the help of these modern imaging techniques, the Vatican Observatory has made significant contributions to the study of stellar evolution, the search for dark matter, and the understanding of the universe's structure.

Furthermore, the observatory has embraced the power of computer simulations and data analysis techniques. By combining observational data with complex computer models, scientists can simulate and understand the processes that occur in the cosmos. The Vatican Observatory has been actively involved in developing and utilizing these simulations to study stellar evolution, galaxy formation, and the dynamics of the universe.

As astronomy continues to push the boundaries of human knowledge, the Vatican Observatory remains at the forefront of modern observational techniques. By harnessing the power of space-based telescopes, radio astronomy, advanced imaging technologies, and computer simulations, the observatory continues to contribute pioneering research to the field. Whether you are an astronomy buff, a Catholic, or simply fascinated by the wonders of the universe, this subchapter will provide you with an insight into the cutting-edge techniques that have shaped our understanding of the cosmos.

Collaborations with Other Observatories

Throughout its long and illustrious history, the Vatican Observatory has fostered numerous collaborations with other observatories around the world, making invaluable contributions to the field of astronomy. These collaborations have not only enhanced our understanding of the universe but have also exemplified the spirit of cooperation and shared knowledge among scientists and astronomers.

One of the primary reasons for these collaborations is the Vatican Observatory's commitment to advancing scientific research and promoting dialogue between science and faith. By partnering with other observatories, the Vatican Observatory has been able to access a wider range of resources, expertise, and cutting-edge technology, thereby greatly expanding the scope and depth of its research endeavors.

A prominent collaboration that deserves special mention is the Vatican Advanced Technology Telescope[1] (VATT) project, a joint venture between the Vatican Observatory and the University of Arizona's Steward Observatory.

---

1. https://www.as.arizona.edu/vatican-advanced-technology-telescope

This state-of-the-art telescope, situated at the Mount Graham International Observatory in Arizona, has provided astronomers with unprecedented observations and data. The VATT has been instrumental in several groundbreaking discoveries, including the detection of exoplanets and the study of distant galaxies and their evolution. This collaboration has not only furthered our knowledge of the cosmos but has also showcased the Vatican Observatory's dedication to embracing technological advancements in the pursuit of scientific excellence.

Another noteworthy collaboration has been the Vatican Observatory's fruitful partnership with the European Space Agency (ESA). Through joint missions and data sharing initiatives, the Vatican Observatory has made significant contributions to ESA's space exploration programs. One such collaboration led to the inclusion of the Vatican's meteorite collection on board ESA's Rosetta mission, which successfully landed a probe on a comet for the first time in history. This collaboration highlights the Vatican Observatory's commitment to interdisciplinary research and its unique ability to bridge the gap between science and faith.

Collaborations with other observatories have not only enriched the Vatican Observatory's research capabilities but have also enabled the sharing of knowledge and expertise with the broader scientific community. By actively engaging with astronomers and scientists from diverse backgrounds, the Vatican Observatory has fostered a culture of open dialogue and intellectual exchange, promoting scientific progress and understanding.

In conclusion, the Vatican Observatory's collaborations with other observatories have been instrumental in its pioneering contributions to astronomy. These partnerships have expanded the scope of research, facilitated access to cutting-edge technology, and promoted interdisciplinary collaboration. Through its commitment to scientific excellence and dialogue, the Vatican Observatory continues to inspire both amateur astronomers and Catholics alike, proving that the pursuit of knowledge knows no boundaries.

Contributions to Theoretical Astronomy

The field of theoretical astronomy has been greatly enriched by the pioneering contributions of the Vatican Observatory. For centuries, the observatory has played a vital role in advancing our understanding of the universe and its workings. In this subchapter, we will explore some of the notable contributions made by the Vatican Observatory to theoretical astronomy.

One of the key areas where the Vatican Observatory has excelled is in the study of stellar evolution. Through a combination of observational data and theoretical models, astronomers at the Vatican Observatory have made significant breakthroughs in understanding how stars evolve over time. Their research has shed light on the life cycles of various types of stars, from the birth of massive stars in stellar nurseries to their ultimate fate as white dwarfs or even supernovae.

In addition to stellar evolution, the Vatican Observatory has also made significant contributions to the study of galactic dynamics. Their observations and analyses have helped unravel the mysteries of galaxy formation and evolution. By studying the motions of stars and gas within galaxies, researchers at the observatory have been able to develop models that explain the structure and dynamics of these vast cosmic systems.

Furthermore, the Vatican Observatory has been at the forefront of research on cosmology, the study of the origin and evolution of the universe as a whole. Through their observations of the cosmic microwave background radiation, astronomers at the observatory have contributed to our understanding of the Big Bang theory and the early moments of the universe's existence. Their work has helped refine our understanding of the fundamental properties of the universe, such as its age and composition.

For Catholic amateur astronomers, the Vatican Observatory's contributions hold a special significance. The observatory's commitment to both scientific inquiry and the Catholic faith has allowed them to bridge the gap between science and religion. By demonstrating that science and faith can coexist harmoniously, the Vatican Observatory has become a symbol of the compatibility between the two realms.

The Vatican Observatory has made pioneering contributions to theoretical astronomy. From their studies of stellar evolution and galactic dynamics to their research on cosmology, the observatory has deepened our understanding of the universe. For amateur astronomers and Catholics alike, the work of the Vatican Observatory serves as a testament to the compatibility between scientific inquiry and religious faith.

Development of Stellar Evolution Models

The study of stars and their evolution has been a fascinating subject for astronomers throughout history. In recent decades, significant advancements have been made in our understanding of stellar evolution, thanks to the pioneering contributions of the Vatican Observatory. This subchapter explores the development of stellar evolution models and the significant role played by the Vatican Observatory in shaping our understanding of this complex process.

Stellar evolution refers to the life cycle of a star, from its birth to its eventual death. It involves various stages, including the formation of a protostar, main-sequence phase, red giant phase, and ultimately, the fate of the star, whether it becomes a white dwarf, neutron star, or black hole. Understanding these stages and the factors that influence a star's evolution is crucial in unraveling the mysteries of the universe.

The Vatican Observatory has made significant contributions to the development of stellar evolution models over the years. Through extensive research and observations, the astronomers at the Vatican Observatory have collected invaluable data on stars of different masses, temperatures, and ages. This data has been instrumental in refining and expanding our understanding of stellar evolution.

One of the breakthroughs made by the Vatican Observatory is the identification and study of binary star systems. By observing the behavior and interactions of stars in binary systems, astronomers can gain insights into the evolution of individual stars. This research has provided crucial evidence for the existence of stellar evolution and has helped refine existing models.

Another significant contribution of the Vatican Observatory is the development of computer simulations and models that can accurately predict the evolution of stars. By combining observational data with theoretical calculations, astronomers at the Vatican Observatory have been able to create sophisticated models that simulate the complex processes occurring within stars. These models have been instrumental in advancing our understanding of stellar evolution and have been widely adopted by the scientific community.

The Vatican Observatory's contributions to stellar evolution models have not only advanced our scientific knowledge but also shed light on the relationship between science and faith. The pursuit of knowledge and understanding the workings of the universe has always been an integral part of the Catholic tradition. The Vatican Observatory's groundbreaking research serves as a testament to the compatibility of science and religion, promoting dialogue and fostering a deeper appreciation of both disciplines.

The development of stellar evolution models has been a significant area of research for the Vatican Observatory. Through their observations, data collection, and development of sophisticated models, astronomers at the Vatican Observatory have made groundbreaking contributions to our understanding of stellar evolution. These contributions have not only expanded our scientific knowledge but also exemplified the harmonious relationship between faith and science. For amateur astronomers and Catholics alike, the Vatican Observatory's pioneering work in this field is a testament to the enduring quest for knowledge and the wonders of the universe.

The Vatican Observatory and Cosmology

The Vatican Observatory has long been at the forefront of scientific research and its contributions to the field of astronomy are truly pioneering. For centuries, the Catholic Church has recognized the importance of studying the heavens and has supported the pursuit of knowledge in this area. In this subchapter, we will explore the fascinating relationship between the Vatican Observatory and cosmology, shedding light on the significant contributions made by this esteemed institution.

The Vatican Observatory's contributions to cosmology have been nothing short of remarkable. From the early days of its establishment in the late 16th century, the observatory has played a crucial role in advancing our understanding of the universe. Its astronomers have made groundbreaking discoveries, challenging prevailing theories and expanding our knowledge of the cosmos.

One major contribution of the Vatican Observatory to cosmology is its involvement in the study of stellar evolution. Through the use of state-of-the-art telescopes and advanced imaging techniques, the observatory has been able to observe and document the life cycle of stars, unraveling the mysteries of their birth, evolution, and death. These findings have not only enriched our understanding of the universe but also provided valuable insights into the fundamental processes that shape celestial bodies.

Additionally, the Vatican Observatory has made significant strides in the study of dark matter and dark energy. By employing advanced instruments and collaborating with international research institutions, the observatory's scientists have played a key role in unraveling the enigmatic nature of these elusive components of the universe. Their work has helped shed light on the structure and dynamics of the cosmos, challenging conventional theories and paving the way for new understandings of the universe's composition.

Moreover, the Vatican Observatory has actively engaged in the dialogue between science and religion. By promoting the idea that faith and reason are not mutually exclusive, but rather, two complementary paths to truth, the observatory has fostered a fruitful relationship between astronomy and Catholicism. Its commitment to exploring the wonders of the universe through scientific inquiry while maintaining a reverence for the divine has made it a unique and valuable presence in the scientific community.

The Vatican Observatory's contributions to cosmology have been diverse and groundbreaking. From its investigations into stellar evolution to its efforts in studying dark matter and dark energy, the observatory has continually pushed the boundaries of scientific knowledge. Moreover, its commitment to integrating science and faith has made it an invaluable institution for both amateur astronomers and Catholics alike. By exploring the mysteries of the cosmos, the Vatican Observatory continues to inspire and inform, bridging the gap between science and spirituality.

Contributions to Planetary Science

The field of planetary science has been greatly enriched by the pioneering contributions of the Vatican Observatory. Combining a deep passion for astronomy with the profound wisdom of Catholic teachings, the observatory has made significant discoveries and advancements that have captivated both amateur astronomers and Catholics alike.

One of the notable contributions of the Vatican Observatory to planetary science is the exploration and study of meteorites. The observatory has collected and analyzed numerous meteorites, shedding light on the origins of our solar system and the processes that have shaped the planets. These findings have not only expanded our understanding of planetary formation but have also provided valuable insights into the potential for extraterrestrial life.

Another area in which the observatory has made significant contributions is the study of comets. By observing and analyzing the behavior of comets, the Vatican Observatory has contributed to our understanding of their composition, structure, and behavior. This research has offered crucial insights into the formation of the early solar system and the potential for comets to carry the building blocks of life.

In addition to studying celestial bodies within our solar system, the Vatican Observatory has also played a vital role in the exploration of exoplanets. Through the use of advanced telescopes and innovative techniques, the observatory has contributed to the discovery of distant planets orbiting other stars. These discoveries have not only expanded our understanding of the vastness and diversity of the universe but have also fueled the search for habitable worlds beyond our own.

The Vatican Observatory's pioneering contributions to planetary science have not only enriched our scientific knowledge but have also served to bridge the gap between science and faith. By demonstrating the compatibility between scientific exploration and Catholic teachings, the observatory has inspired many to appreciate the wonders of the universe while remaining grounded in their spiritual beliefs.

For amateur astronomers, the Vatican Observatory's contributions to planetary science offer a fascinating glimpse into the mysteries of the universe. From the study of meteorites to the exploration of exoplanets, the observatory's research has pushed the boundaries of our knowledge and sparked new avenues of inquiry.

For Catholics, the Vatican Observatory's work serves as a testament to the Church's commitment to the pursuit of knowledge and the harmony between faith and reason. By actively engaging in scientific research, the observatory encourages Catholics to embrace the beauty and complexity of the natural world while deepening their understanding of God's creation.

The Vatican Observatory's contributions to planetary science have had a profound impact on both the field of astronomy and the Catholic community. From meteorites to comets and exoplanets, the observatory's work has expanded our knowledge of the universe while inspiring a sense of wonder and awe in the hearts and minds of amateur astronomers and Catholics alike.

The Vatican Observatory's Impact on Astronomy Education and Outreach

The Vatican Observatory has made significant contributions to the field of astronomy throughout its long and storied history. However, its impact goes beyond scientific research. The observatory has played a crucial role in astronomy education and outreach, leaving a lasting impression on both amateur astronomers and Catholics.

One of the most notable ways the Vatican Observatory has impacted astronomy education is through its dedication to promoting the study of science within the Catholic Church. With the establishment of the Vatican Observatory Foundation, the institution has been able to support research and educational programs that bridge the gap between faith and science. By fostering dialogue and understanding between the two realms, the Vatican

Observatory has encouraged many Catholics to pursue astronomy and related sciences.

The Vatican Observatory has also been instrumental in reaching out to the general public and sharing the wonders of the universe with astronomy enthusiasts. Through its numerous outreach programs, the observatory has organized public lectures, stargazing events, and astronomy workshops. These initiatives have not only educated the public about the latest discoveries in astronomy but have also inspired many individuals to explore the field further. The observatory has successfully made astronomy accessible to people of all ages and backgrounds, nurturing a sense of wonder and curiosity about the cosmos.

Moreover, the Vatican Observatory has made significant contributions to astronomy education by publishing research papers, books, and articles. These publications have not only advanced scientific knowledge but have also served as valuable educational resources for astronomy enthusiasts and students. By disseminating their research findings, the observatory has become a reliable source of information for those interested in both astronomy and Catholic perspectives on the universe.

The impact of the Vatican Observatory on astronomy education and outreach is far-reaching and enduring. By fostering an appreciation for science within the Catholic community and engaging the public through various initiatives, the observatory has encouraged countless individuals to explore the wonders of the universe. Whether through public events, publications, or educational programs, the Vatican Observatory has played a vital role in promoting astronomy and inspiring generations of amateur astronomers, Catholics, and enthusiasts from all walks of life.

Vatican Observatory Summer Schools

The Vatican Observatory Summer Schools[2] are an integral part of the Vatican Observatory's mission to bridge the gap between faith and science. These unique educational programs bring together amateur astronomers and

---

2. https://www.vaticanobservatory.va/en/education/voss

Catholics from around the world to explore the contributions of the Vatican Observatory to the field of astronomy.

For amateur astronomers, the Vatican Observatory Summer Schools offer an unparalleled opportunity to learn from some of the brightest minds in the field. The program brings together renowned astronomers, astrophysicists, and theologians who have made significant contributions to our understanding of the universe. Participants have the chance to engage in stimulating discussions, attend lectures, and even conduct research alongside these experts.

Catholics, in particular, find these summer schools to be a transformative experience. The Vatican Observatory's commitment to the harmony between faith and science resonates deeply with their beliefs. By delving into the fascinating world of astronomy, participants gain a deeper appreciation for the wonders of creation and the role that science plays in understanding God's plan.

The summer schools cover a wide range of topics, including cosmology, astrophysics, and the history of astronomy. Participants explore the cutting-edge research conducted at the Vatican Observatory, which has made significant contributions to the field. From studying the origins of the universe to examining the latest advancements in telescopic technology, attendees gain a comprehensive understanding of the evolving nature of astronomy.

In addition to the intellectual pursuits, the Vatican Observatory Summer Schools also provide a unique cultural experience. Participants have the opportunity to immerse themselves in the rich history and art of Rome, visiting iconic sites such as the Vatican Museums and St. Peter's Basilica. These excursions enhance the overall experience and create lasting memories.

Whether you are an astronomy buff, a Catholic seeking to explore the intersection of faith and science, or simply someone fascinated by the Vatican Observatory's contributions to astronomy, the Vatican Observatory Summer Schools offer a transformative and enriching experience. Join us in this incredible journey of discovery and witness firsthand the harmonious relationship between science and faith.

Public Lectures and Exhibitions

The Vatican Observatory has long been renowned for its groundbreaking contributions to the field of astronomy. However, its impact does not stop at the scientific community. Recognizing the importance of sharing knowledge and fostering public interest, the observatory regularly organizes public lectures and exhibitions to engage with amateur astronomers and Catholics alike.

These public lectures serve as a platform for the Vatican Observatory to showcase its pioneering contributions to the field of astronomy. By bringing together renowned astronomers, scientists, and experts, these events provide a unique opportunity for attendees to learn about the observatory's groundbreaking discoveries and advancements. From the exploration of distant galaxies to the study of exoplanets, these lectures offer a glimpse into the fascinating world of Catholic astronomy.

The lectures are carefully designed to cater to both amateur astronomers and Catholics, ensuring that the content is accessible and engaging for a diverse audience. Whether you are an ardent follower of the cosmos or someone seeking to deepen their understanding of the intersection between science and faith, these lectures offer a thought-provoking experience. The speakers not only present scientific findings but also delve into the theological and philosophical implications of the observatory's work, highlighting the harmony between science and Catholicism.

In addition to lectures, the Vatican Observatory also hosts exhibitions that bring astronomy to life. These exhibitions showcase rare astronomical artifacts, including antique telescopes, astrolabes, and celestial maps. Visitors have the opportunity to explore the history of astronomy and witness how the Vatican Observatory's contributions have shaped our understanding of the universe. Interactive displays and multimedia presentations further enhance the experience, allowing attendees to engage with the exhibits on a deeper level.

These public lectures and exhibitions play a crucial role in promoting the contributions of the Vatican Observatory to astronomy. By reaching out to a wider audience, the observatory aims to ignite curiosity, inspire awe, and foster a deeper appreciation for the wonders of the universe. Whether you are a devout Catholic, an avid astronomy enthusiast, or simply curious about the intersection of science and faith, these events offer a unique opportunity to explore the groundbreaking work of the Vatican Observatory and its enduring impact on our understanding of the cosmos.

Collaborative Projects with Educational Institutions

One of the key factors that have contributed to the success and pioneering contributions of the Vatican Observatory in the field of astronomy is its collaborative projects with various educational institutions. By partnering with top universities and research centers around the world, the Vatican Observatory has been able to expand its research capabilities and share its knowledge with a wider audience.

These collaborative projects have allowed the Vatican Observatory to tap into the expertise and resources of leading educational institutions, enabling them to conduct cutting-edge research and make significant advancements in the field of astronomy. Through these partnerships, the Vatican Observatory has been able to access state-of-the-art equipment, telescopes, and observatories, which have played a crucial role in their groundbreaking discoveries.

Furthermore, these collaborations have facilitated the exchange of ideas and knowledge between the Vatican Observatory and other experts in the field. By joining forces with renowned astronomers and scientists, the Vatican Observatory has been able to benefit from their expertise, while also contributing its own unique insights and perspectives. This cross-pollination of ideas has resulted in a rich and diverse body of research, leading to a deeper understanding of the universe.

Additionally, the collaborative projects with educational institutions have helped the Vatican Observatory to fulfill its mission of promoting education and outreach in astronomy. By working closely with universities and research centers, the Vatican Observatory has been able to develop educational programs and initiatives that cater to both amateur astronomers and Catholics interested in the field. These programs provide opportunities for individuals to learn about the contributions of the Vatican Observatory to astronomy and engage in meaningful discussions on the intersection of science and faith.

In conclusion, the collaborative projects with educational institutions have been instrumental in the Vatican Observatory's pioneering contributions to the field of astronomy. Through these partnerships, the Observatory has been able to leverage the expertise and resources of leading institutions, foster the exchange of knowledge, and promote education and outreach in astronomy. These collaborations have not only enhanced the Observatory's research capabilities but have also allowed them to share their discoveries and insights with a wider audience, fulfilling their mission of advancing the frontiers of knowledge and fostering dialogue between science and faith.

Chapter 3: The Vatican Observatory's Groundbreaking Discoveries

"Unlocking the Celestial Vault: Journeying Through the Vatican Observatory's Trailblazing Discoveries"

Exploring the Solar System

The Solar System, with its countless celestial bodies and mesmerizing mysteries, has captivated humanity for centuries. In this subchapter, we delve into the intriguing world of our cosmic neighborhood, shedding light on the Vatican Observatory's pioneering contributions to unlocking its secrets. This exploration will surely appeal to amateur astronomers, Catholics, and those interested in the remarkable contributions of the Vatican Observatory to the field of astronomy.

The Solar System, spanning an unimaginable expanse of 4.6 billion years, is home to our beloved planet Earth and a plethora of other celestial objects. The Vatican Observatory, a leading institution in astronomical research, has played a crucial role in unraveling the enigmatic nature of our solar neighborhood. From studying the movements of planets to the search for life beyond our planet, the Vatican Observatory has made significant contributions, bridging the gap between science and faith.

One of the most remarkable contributions is the extensive research conducted on the dynamics and behavior of comets and asteroids. By observing these celestial wanderers, the Vatican Observatory has not only enhanced our understanding of their origins but has also contributed to the advancement of planetary defense strategies. This research has proven invaluable in protecting our planet from potential catastrophic collisions, highlighting the Vatican Observatory's commitment to the well-being of humanity.

Furthermore, the Vatican Observatory has been at the forefront of studying the Sun, our nearest star. By employing cutting-edge telescopes and technology, the observatory has made groundbreaking discoveries about the Sun's behavior, including solar flares, sunspots, and solar wind. This research has not only deepened our understanding of our star but has also shed light on the intricate interplay between the Sun and Earth's climate, contributing to global efforts in climate science.

Moreover, the Vatican Observatory's commitment to the exploration of our neighboring planets is noteworthy. Through collaborative missions with space agencies worldwide, the observatory has contributed to the understanding of Mars, Venus, and other celestial bodies in our Solar System. By analyzing their geological compositions, atmospheric conditions, and potential for sustaining life, the Vatican Observatory has furthered our knowledge of the universe and its potential for harboring life.

In conclusion, the subchapter "Exploring the Solar System" offers a captivating journey through the Vatican Observatory's pioneering contributions to the realm of astronomy. From deciphering the secrets of comets and asteroids to unraveling the dynamics of our nearest star, the Vatican Observatory's research has enriched our understanding of the Solar System. Aimed at amateur astronomers and Catholics, this subchapter provides a unique perspective on the contributions of the Vatican Observatory, bridging the gap between science and faith, and inspiring a sense of wonder about our cosmic neighborhood.

Discoveries in Planetary Astronomy

The field of planetary astronomy has witnessed numerous groundbreaking discoveries over the years, unraveling the mysteries of the celestial bodies that populate our solar system. In this subchapter, we delve into some of the remarkable findings in planetary astronomy and explore the pioneering contributions of the Vatican Observatory to this fascinating field.

One of the most significant discoveries in planetary astronomy is the detection of exoplanets, which are planets located outside our solar system. The Vatican Observatory has played a pivotal role in this area of research, contributing to the identification and characterization of these distant worlds. Through the use of advanced telescopes and sophisticated instruments, astronomers at the Vatican Observatory have been able to detect exoplanets by observing slight variations in the light emitted by their parent stars. This breakthrough has expanded our understanding of planetary systems beyond our own, leading to the realization that our solar system is just one among countless others.

Another remarkable discovery is the existence of water on other celestial bodies within our solar system. The Vatican Observatory has contributed to the study of water ice on the Moon, Mars, and Jupiter's moon Europa. By analyzing data from spacecraft missions and ground-based observations, scientists have found evidence of subsurface ice on these planetary bodies, suggesting the possibility of past or even present microbial life. These findings have fueled speculation about the potential habitability of other worlds and paved the way for future exploration missions.

Furthermore, the Vatican Observatory has made significant strides in the study of asteroids and comets, shedding light on their origins and compositions. Through spectroscopic analysis and close observations, astronomers have discovered valuable insights into the formation of these celestial bodies and their potential impact on Earth. This research has not only deepened our knowledge of the solar system's early history but also contributed to efforts to safeguard our planet from potential asteroid impacts.

The field of planetary astronomy has witnessed remarkable discoveries that have revolutionized our understanding of the universe. The pioneering contributions of the Vatican Observatory to this field have been instrumental in unraveling the mysteries of exoplanets, water on other celestial bodies, and the origins of asteroids and comets. By merging scientific inquiry with the teachings of the Catholic faith, the Vatican Observatory continues to inspire amateur astronomers and Catholics alike, fostering a deeper appreciation for the wonders of the cosmos and the harmony between science and spirituality.

Vatican Observatory's Role in the Study of Comets and Asteroids

The Vatican Observatory, with its rich history and pioneering contributions to the field of astronomy, has played a significant role in the study of comets and asteroids. In this subchapter, we will delve into the specific ways in which the Vatican Observatory has contributed to our understanding of these celestial bodies.

Comets and asteroids have long fascinated astronomers and have provided crucial insights into the formation and evolution of our solar system. The Vatican Observatory has actively participated in the observation, tracking, and analysis of these celestial objects, significantly advancing our knowledge in this area.

One of the key contributions of the Vatican Observatory in the study of comets and asteroids is its extensive observational research. Equipped with state-of-the-art telescopes and advanced instruments, the observatory has conducted systematic observations of these objects, aiding in the identification and tracking of their trajectories. This research has helped astronomers understand the composition, physical properties, and behavior of comets and asteroids.

Furthermore, the Vatican Observatory has been at the forefront of efforts to catalog and monitor near-Earth objects (NEOs). These are asteroids and comets that have orbits that bring them in close proximity to our planet. By collaborating with international organizations dedicated to NEO detection and tracking, the observatory has contributed to the identification of potentially hazardous objects, thus playing a vital role in planetary defense.

In addition to observational research, the Vatican Observatory has also contributed to theoretical studies on the origin and evolution of comets and asteroids. By combining observational data with theoretical models, astronomers at the observatory have made significant strides in understanding the formation processes of these objects and their relationship to the early solar system.

The Vatican Observatory's commitment to integrating faith and reason also makes its contributions unique. By bridging the gap between science and religion, the observatory offers a holistic approach to the study of comets and asteroids. This approach encourages dialogue between astronomers and theologians, fostering a deeper understanding of the universe and its significance.

The Vatican Observatory has made substantial contributions to the study of comets and asteroids. Through its observational research, cataloging efforts, theoretical studies, and unique approach, the observatory has significantly advanced our understanding of these celestial bodies. amateur astronomers and Catholics alike can appreciate the groundbreaking work of the Vatican Observatory in unraveling the mysteries of comets and asteroids, bringing us closer to a deeper understanding of our origins and place in the cosmos.

Deep Space Exploration

Humanity's fascination with the vastness of the universe has propelled us to embark on a journey of deep space exploration. The Vatican Observatory, known for its pioneering contributions, has played a significant role in unraveling the mysteries of the cosmos. This subchapter delves into the fascinating realm of deep space exploration and highlights the remarkable contributions made by the Vatican Observatory.

Deep space exploration involves venturing beyond the confines of our solar system to study celestial objects such as galaxies, nebulae, and black holes. The Vatican Observatory has been at the forefront of this endeavor, employing state-of-the-art telescopes, innovative technologies, and a team of dedicated scientists to explore the wonders of the universe.

One of the remarkable contributions of the Vatican Observatory to deep space exploration is its involvement in the study of distant galaxies. Through the use of powerful telescopes, astronomers at the observatory have observed and analyzed countless galaxies, shedding light on their formation, evolution, and various phenomena occurring within them. Their research has significantly expanded our understanding of the universe's structure and the processes that shape it.

Furthermore, the Vatican Observatory's pioneering contributions to the study of nebulae have been invaluable. Nebulae, sprawling clouds of gas and dust, offer a glimpse into the birth and death of stars. By meticulously studying these celestial phenomena, the observatory has contributed to our knowledge of stellar evolution, the formation of planetary systems, and the intricate interplay of cosmic forces.

Moreover, the exploration of black holes, enigmatic yet powerful entities, has been a focal point of the Vatican Observatory's research. These celestial objects possess gravitational forces so strong that nothing, not even light, can escape their grasp. Through advanced observational techniques and collaborations with international partners, the observatory has made significant strides in unraveling the mysteries surrounding black holes, offering crucial insights into their formation, behavior, and effects on the surrounding cosmos.

For amateur astronomers and Catholics alike, the Vatican Observatory's contributions to deep space exploration are a testament to the harmonious coexistence of faith and science. By exploring the wonders of the universe, the observatory fosters a deeper appreciation for the grandeur of God's creation while simultaneously advancing our scientific understanding.

Deep space exploration is an awe-inspiring journey that pushes the boundaries of human knowledge. The Vatican Observatory's pioneering contributions to this field have been instrumental in expanding our understanding of distant galaxies, nebulae, and black holes. By shedding light on the mysteries of the cosmos, the observatory serves as a bridge between faith and science, captivating amateur astronomers and Catholics alike.

Contributions to Galactic Astronomy

Galactic astronomy, the study of our Milky Way galaxy and its various components, has been an area of significant interest and research for astronomers throughout history. In this subchapter, we will explore the pioneering contributions made by the Vatican Observatory to the field of galactic astronomy.

The Vatican Observatory, with its rich Catholic heritage and commitment to scientific exploration, has played a crucial role in advancing our understanding of the Milky Way galaxy. Since its establishment in 1891, the observatory has been at the forefront of scientific research, consistently contributing valuable insights and groundbreaking discoveries.

One of the notable contributions of the Vatican Observatory to galactic astronomy is the study of stellar populations within the Milky Way. By examining the composition, distribution, and evolution of stars, astronomers at the Vatican Observatory have shed light on the formation and dynamics of our galaxy. Their meticulous observations and analysis have provided crucial data for constructing accurate models of the Milky Way's structure and understanding its intricate web of stars.

Another area of significant contribution is the exploration of galactic interstellar matter. The Vatican Observatory has contributed to understanding the distribution and properties of interstellar gas and dust, which are essential components for star formation. Through spectroscopic observations and innovative techniques, they have unraveled the complex nature of interstellar matter, deciphering its role in shaping the evolution of galaxies.

Furthermore, the Vatican Observatory has made notable contributions to the study of variable stars, which are stars that exhibit changes in brightness over time. By monitoring and studying these stellar phenomena, astronomers have gained insights into the physical processes occurring within stars, their lifecycles, and the role they play in galactic evolution. The observatory's long-term monitoring programs have provided valuable data for understanding the behavior of variable stars and their impact on the overall galactic structure.

The Vatican Observatory's pioneering contributions to galactic astronomy have significantly enriched our understanding of the Milky Way galaxy. Their research on stellar populations, interstellar matter, and variable stars has provided valuable insights into the formation, dynamics, and evolution of galaxies. By combining their Catholic heritage with scientific exploration, the Vatican Observatory continues to make significant strides in unraveling the mysteries of the universe and inspiring both amateur astronomers and Catholics alike.

Vatican Observatory's Research on Extragalactic Objects

The Vatican Observatory has been at the forefront of astronomical research for centuries, making pioneering contributions that have significantly advanced our understanding of the universe. One area of research in which the observatory has made significant strides is the study of extragalactic objects.

Extragalactic objects refer to objects located outside our Milky Way galaxy. These objects include galaxies, quasars, and other celestial bodies that exist in vast distances from our own cosmic neighborhood. The study of these objects is crucial for understanding the structure, evolution, and dynamics of the universe on a larger scale.

The Vatican Observatory's research on extragalactic objects has been revolutionary in many ways. Through the use of advanced telescopes and innovative observational techniques, the observatory has played a pivotal role in uncovering the mysteries of these distant cosmic entities.

One of the most significant contributions of the Vatican Observatory in this field is its involvement in the Hubble Space Telescope project. The observatory has been actively engaged in the planning, execution, and analysis of observations made by this groundbreaking telescope. The data collected by the Hubble Space Telescope has provided astronomers with unparalleled insights into the nature of extragalactic objects, their formation, and their interaction with their surroundings.

Moreover, the Vatican Observatory has also conducted extensive research on active galactic nuclei (AGNs) and quasars. These incredibly energetic and distant objects have been a subject of great interest for astronomers, as they offer a unique window into the early universe and the processes that govern its evolution. Through detailed observations and analysis of AGNs and quasars, the observatory has made significant contributions to our understanding of the mechanisms that drive their immense energy output, as well as their role in shaping the cosmos.

The Vatican Observatory's research on extragalactic objects has not only expanded our knowledge of the universe but has also showcased the compatibility between faith and science. By actively participating in cutting-edge astronomical research, the observatory reaffirms the Catholic Church's commitment to exploring the wonders of the natural world and the harmony between science and religion.

For amateur astronomers and Catholics alike, the Vatican Observatory's contributions to the study of extragalactic objects serve as a testament to the power of human curiosity and the limitless potential of scientific exploration. Through its pioneering research, the observatory continues to inspire and educate, bridging the gaps between scientific discovery, faith, and the wonders of the cosmos.

Discoveries in the Field of Cosmology

Cosmology, the study of the origin, evolution, and structure of the universe, has captivated the minds of astronomers and enthusiasts alike for centuries. In this subchapter, we delve into the fascinating discoveries made in the field of cosmology, with a particular focus on the pioneering contributions of the Vatican Observatory.

The Vatican Observatory, established in 1891, has played a crucial role in unraveling the mysteries of the cosmos. Through its dedicated astronomers and cutting-edge research, it has made significant strides in expanding our understanding of the universe.

One of the most profound discoveries in cosmology is the concept of the Big Bang. The Vatican Observatory, through its observations and collaborations with other renowned institutions, has provided valuable insights into this theory. By studying the cosmic microwave background radiation, a remnant of the early universe, astronomers have been able to support the idea that the universe originated from a single, explosive event billions of years ago.

Another breakthrough in cosmology is the discovery of dark matter and dark energy. The Vatican Observatory has been actively involved in the investigation of these elusive components that make up the majority of the universe. Through meticulous observations and data analysis, astronomers have postulated the existence of dark matter, which exerts gravitational forces but cannot be directly detected. Dark energy, on the other hand, is believed to be responsible for the accelerated expansion of the universe. By studying the distribution of galaxies and the cosmic microwave background, the Vatican Observatory has contributed to our understanding of these enigmatic phenomena.

Moreover, the Vatican Observatory has also made significant contributions to the study of exoplanets, planets that orbit stars outside our solar system. This field of research has revolutionized our understanding of the potential for extraterrestrial life. By utilizing advanced telescopes and techniques, astronomers have discovered numerous exoplanets, some of which may have the conditions necessary to support life. The Vatican Observatory's role in these discoveries highlights the compatibility of astronomy and faith, as it explores the vastness of the universe and the possibility of life beyond Earth.

The Vatican Observatory has made pioneering contributions to the field of cosmology, shedding light on the origins and composition of the universe. By studying the Big Bang, dark matter, dark energy, and exoplanets, the observatory has pushed the boundaries of human knowledge and deepened our appreciation for the wonders of creation. For amateur astronomers and Catholics alike, this subchapter provides an insightful glimpse into the Vatican Observatory's remarkable achievements and its ongoing quest to unravel the mysteries of the cosmos.

Unveiling the Mysteries of the Universe

The exploration of the universe has captivated humanity for centuries. From ancient civilizations gazing at the stars in wonder to modern-day astronomers peering through advanced telescopes, the quest to unravel the mysteries of the universe has been an ongoing endeavor. In the realm of astronomy, the Vatican Observatory's pioneering contributions have played a significant role in advancing our understanding of the cosmos.

For amateur astronomers and Catholics alike, the subchapter titled "Unveiling the Mysteries of the Universe" in the book "Catholic Astronomy: The Vatican Observatory's Pioneering Contributions" offers an insightful journey into the profound discoveries made by the Vatican Observatory.

The Vatican Observatory, founded in 1891 by Pope Leo XIII, has been at the forefront of astronomical research for over a century. Its mission, to bridge the gap between science and faith, has led to groundbreaking contributions in various areas of astronomy. This subchapter delves into the remarkable achievements made by the Observatory, focusing on its significant contributions to the field.

One of the key areas of focus for the Vatican Observatory has been stellar evolution. Through meticulous observations and cutting-edge research, the Observatory has shed light on the life cycles of stars, from their birth in stellar nurseries to their spectacular deaths as supernovae. These findings have not only deepened our understanding of the universe but have also sparked philosophical and theological reflections on the wonder of creation.

Another area where the Vatican Observatory has made pioneering contributions is in the study of exoplanets. The Observatory has actively participated in the search for planets beyond our solar system, employing innovative techniques to detect and characterize these distant worlds. By expanding our knowledge of exoplanets, the Vatican Observatory has provided valuable insights into the potential for extraterrestrial life and the implications it may have for our understanding of God's creation.

Furthermore, the subchapter explores the Vatican Observatory's involvement in cosmology, the study of the origin, evolution, and structure of the universe. Through collaborations with prominent scientists and the utilization of advanced telescopes, the Observatory has made significant contributions to our understanding of the Big Bang theory, dark matter, and dark energy – fundamental components that shape the cosmos as we know it.

For amateur astronomers, Catholics, and those intrigued by the contributions of the Vatican Observatory to the field, "Unveiling the Mysteries of the Universe" provides an engaging and enlightening exploration of the groundbreaking research conducted by this unique institution. From stars to exoplanets and the vast expanse of the universe, this subchapter offers a glimpse into the profound discoveries that have captivated the minds and hearts of astronomers and believers alike.

Vatican Observatory's Contributions to Stellar Astrophysics

The Vatican Observatory has long been recognized as a pioneering institution in the field of astronomy, and its contributions to stellar astrophysics are particularly noteworthy. Combining the scientific rigor of astrophysics with the spiritual perspective of the Catholic Church, the observatory has made significant advancements in understanding the nature of stars and the processes that govern their evolution.

One of the key areas of research conducted by the Vatican Observatory is the study of stellar evolution. Through meticulous observations and data analysis, the observatory's astronomers have contributed to our understanding of the life cycles of stars, from their birth in massive interstellar clouds to their eventual death as supernovae or white dwarfs. This research has helped to refine models of stellar evolution and shed light on the processes that drive the formation of stars and galaxies.

Another important contribution of the Vatican Observatory to stellar astrophysics is the study of variable stars. By monitoring the brightness fluctuations of these stars over time, astronomers can gain insights into their physical properties and uncover important clues about the underlying astrophysical mechanisms at work. The observatory's extensive observations of variable stars have provided valuable data for the development of models that explain their behavior, such as pulsation and eclipsing binary systems.

Furthermore, the Vatican Observatory has played a crucial role in the study of stellar spectroscopy. By analyzing the light emitted by stars across different wavelengths, astronomers can determine their chemical composition, temperature, and other fundamental properties. The observatory's spectroscopic observations have contributed to the development of spectral classification systems, which are used to categorize stars based on their spectral features. This classification system has been instrumental in understanding the diversity of stars and their evolutionary paths.

In addition to these scientific contributions, the Vatican Observatory has also fostered dialogue between science and faith. By integrating scientific research with theological reflection, the observatory has shown that there is no inherent conflict between science and religion. On the contrary, the pursuit of scientific knowledge can deepen our understanding of God's creation and inspire a sense of awe and wonder.

The Vatican Observatory's contributions to stellar astrophysics have been significant and far-reaching. Through its research on stellar evolution, variable stars, and spectroscopy, the observatory has enriched our understanding of the universe and its mysteries. Moreover, by bridging the gap between science and faith, it has provided a unique perspective that appeals to both amateur astronomers and Catholics alike.

Research on Supernovae and Stellar Explosions

The study of supernovae and stellar explosions has always captivated the human imagination. These awe-inspiring events have the power to shape the cosmos, leaving astronomers and astrophysicists eager to unravel their mysteries. In the realm of Catholic astronomy, the Vatican Observatory has made pioneering contributions to understanding these cosmic cataclysms, shedding light on the intricate workings of the universe.

Supernovae, the spectacular explosions of massive stars, mark the end of a stellar life cycle. They release an immense amount of energy, outshining entire galaxies for a brief period. The Vatican Observatory has been at the forefront of research on supernovae, employing cutting-edge telescopes and scientific techniques to observe and analyze these remarkable phenomena. By studying the light emitted during a supernova explosion, scientists can decipher the elements produced in the explosion, uncovering the processes that lead to the creation of heavy elements essential for life itself.

One of the significant contributions of the Vatican Observatory to the field of supernova research is the development of advanced spectrographs. These instruments allow astronomers to split the light from a supernova into its constituent colors, providing crucial information about the composition, temperature, and velocity of the ejected material. Through their observations, Vatican astronomers have refined our understanding of the different types of supernovae, such as Type Ia, which are used as "standard candles" to measure cosmic distances.

Stellar explosions not only provide insights into the evolution of stars but also serve as laboratories for studying fundamental physics. By observing the remnants of supernovae, such as pulsars and black holes, scientists can probe the extremes of gravity and test Einstein's theory of general relativity. The Vatican Observatory has made significant contributions to this field, contributing to our understanding of neutron stars and the nature of black holes.

For Catholic astronomers and astronomy enthusiasts alike, the Vatican Observatory's research on supernovae and stellar explosions offers a unique perspective. It combines the awe-inspiring beauty of the cosmos with the intellectual rigor of scientific inquiry, demonstrating the compatibility of faith and reason. By exploring the mysteries of the universe, the Vatican Observatory invites Catholics to marvel at the grandeur of God's creation while deepening their appreciation for the wonders of the cosmos.

The Vatican Observatory's pioneering research on supernovae and stellar explosions has enriched our understanding of the universe and its origins. With their advanced instruments and deep commitment to scientific inquiry, Vatican astronomers have made significant contributions to the field of astronomy. For amateur astronomers, Catholics, and those interested in the contributions of the Vatican Observatory, the study of supernovae and stellar explosions serves as a gateway to explore the intersection of faith and science, inspiring a sense of wonder and awe for the cosmos.

Vatican Observatory's Role in Unraveling Dark Matter and Dark Energy

In the fascinating realm of astronomy, there are few mysteries as captivating as dark matter and dark energy. These enigmatic entities have puzzled scientists for decades, but thanks to the pioneering contributions of the Vatican Observatory, we have made significant strides in unraveling their secrets.

For amateur astronomers and Catholics alike, understanding the role of the Vatican Observatory in this field is essential. Established in 1891 by Pope Leo XIII, the observatory has been at the forefront of astronomical research, combining faith and science to explore the wonders of the universe.

Dark matter, often referred to as the "invisible glue" of the cosmos, is a hypothetical form of matter that does not interact with light or other electromagnetic radiation. Its existence was first postulated to explain the gravitational forces acting on galaxies and galaxy clusters. The Vatican Observatory has made significant contributions to the study of dark matter, particularly through its collaboration with leading astrophysicists and cosmologists. By using advanced telescopes and spectrographs, researchers at the observatory have helped refine our understanding of dark matter's distribution in galaxies and its role in shaping the large-scale structure of the universe.

Dark energy, on the other hand, is an even more mysterious concept. It is believed to be responsible for the accelerated expansion of the universe. The Vatican Observatory has played a crucial role in studying dark energy by conducting extensive observations of distant supernovae. These observations, combined with data from other international collaborations, have provided strong evidence for the existence of dark energy and its profound influence on cosmic expansion.

Beyond its scientific contributions, the Vatican Observatory's involvement in unraveling dark matter and dark energy aligns with the Catholic Church's commitment to promoting dialogue between faith and reason. By exploring the mysteries of the universe, the observatory demonstrates that scientific inquiry and religious belief can coexist harmoniously.

The Vatican Observatory's pioneering contributions to astronomy have significantly advanced our understanding of dark matter and dark energy. For amateur astronomers and Catholics interested in the intersection of science and faith, delving into the observatory's role in unraveling these cosmic mysteries is both enlightening and awe-inspiring. Through its research and collaboration, the Vatican Observatory continues to inspire curiosity and deepen our appreciation for the wonders of the universe.

Chapter 4: The Vatican Observatory and Faith-Science Dialogue

"Bridging the Cosmos and the Divine: The Vatican Observatory's Journey in Harmonizing Faith and Science"

The Vatican Observatory's Approach to Faith-Science Integration

In the realm of science and religion, few institutions have managed to navigate the complex landscape as successfully as the Vatican Observatory. Founded in 1891, the Observatory has made pioneering contributions to the field of astronomy while remaining firmly rooted in the Catholic faith. This subchapter explores the unique approach adopted by the Vatican Observatory in integrating faith and science, offering a fascinating glimpse into the harmonious coexistence of these seemingly disparate domains.

At its core, the Vatican Observatory's approach to faith-science integration is grounded in the belief that the study of the natural world can deepen our understanding of God's creation. Rather than viewing science as a threat to religious faith, the Observatory sees it as a means of uncovering the wonders of the universe and appreciating the divine intelligence behind it. This perspective allows for a seamless integration of scientific inquiry and religious contemplation, fostering a profound sense of awe and reverence for both.

The Vatican Observatory's commitment to faith-science integration is evident in its scholarly pursuits. The institution has played a significant role in advancing our understanding of the cosmos, contributing to fields such as stellar evolution, galactic dynamics, and cosmology. Through rigorous scientific research, the Observatory seeks to unravel the mysteries of the universe while acknowledging that these discoveries are ultimately a testament to the grandeur of God's creation.

Beyond its scientific endeavors, the Vatican Observatory actively promotes dialogue between faith and science. It recognizes that both disciplines have valuable insights to offer and that a fruitful exchange can enrich our understanding of the universe and our place within it. The Observatory organizes conferences and seminars where scientists, theologians, and philosophers come together to engage in meaningful discussions, exploring the intersections between science, faith, and philosophy.

For amateur astronomers, the Vatican Observatory's approach provides a unique perspective, offering an opportunity to explore the wonders of the universe through the lens of faith. By delving into the Observatory's pioneering contributions to astronomy, readers can gain a deeper appreciation for the marriage of science and religion and the profound insights that can emerge from their harmonious coexistence.

Catholics, in particular, will find inspiration in the Vatican Observatory's approach. It reinforces the idea that science is not antithetical to religious belief but rather an avenue through which to deepen one's understanding of God's creation. The Observatory's work serves as a powerful testament to the compatibility of faith and science, encouraging Catholics to embrace both disciplines and view them as complementary aspects of a holistic worldview.

The Vatican Observatory's approach to faith-science integration is an exemplar of harmonious coexistence. By recognizing the inherent value in both scientific inquiry and religious contemplation, the Observatory has made pioneering contributions to astronomy while remaining firmly rooted in the Catholic faith. amateur astronomers and Catholics alike can draw inspiration from this unique approach, appreciating the profound insights that emerge from the marriage of science and religion.

Implications of Catholic Teachings on Astronomy

The intersection between Catholic teachings and the field of astronomy is a fascinating area of exploration. For centuries, the Catholic Church has played a significant role in the study and understanding of the cosmos. In this subchapter, we will delve into the implications of Catholic teachings on astronomy, shedding light on the unique perspectives and contributions of the Vatican Observatory.

Catholic teachings on astronomy are rooted in the belief that the universe is a manifestation of God's creation. The Church has long encouraged the pursuit of knowledge and the exploration of the natural world, including the study of celestial bodies. This perspective has had profound implications for astronomy, shaping the way Catholic astronomers approach their research.

One of the key implications is the emphasis on the harmony between faith and reason. Catholic teachings encourage Catholics to seek a deeper understanding of the natural world while also recognizing the existence of a higher power. This approach has allowed Catholic astronomers to engage in scientific inquiry while maintaining a spiritual perspective.

Another implication is the recognition of the inherent beauty and awe-inspiring nature of the universe. Catholic teachings highlight the idea that the cosmos is not merely a collection of random objects but rather a reflection of God's design. This perspective has inspired Catholic astronomers to study and appreciate the celestial wonders with a sense of wonder and reverence.

The Vatican Observatory's pioneering contributions to astronomy have further shaped the implications of Catholic teachings. Established in 1891, the Vatican Observatory has been at the forefront of astronomical research, blending scientific rigor with a deep respect for religious beliefs. Its astronomers have made significant discoveries and advancements, contributing to our understanding of the universe.

Catholic teachings encourage believers to appreciate the wonders of creation. The vastness of the universe, celestial bodies, and the intricate laws governing the cosmos are seen as expressions of God's creativity. This appreciation encourages a sense of awe and wonder at the complexity and beauty of the universe.

The observatory's contributions include the study of stellar evolution, cosmology, and the search for exoplanets. These scientific endeavors are guided by the conviction that understanding the natural world is a way to deepen our appreciation for God's creation. Catholic teachings acknowledge the value of scientific inquiry as a means of exploring the natural order. The Church supports scientific endeavors, including astronomical research, recognizing that the pursuit of knowledge enriches human understanding and contributes to the common good.

While supporting scientific inquiry, Catholic teachings recognize the limits of human knowledge. The mysteries of the cosmos and the questions surrounding the origins and nature of the universe are viewed with humility. This acknowledgment encourages a sense of reverence for the mysteries that transcend human understanding.

Catholic teachings underscore the interconnectedness of all creation. This perspective extends to the cosmic realm, emphasizing that the study of astronomy contributes to a holistic understanding of the universe as part of God's intricate design.

The implications of Catholic teachings on astronomy are profound and far-reaching. The emphasis on the harmony between faith and reason, the recognition of the beauty of the cosmos, and the pioneering contributions of the Vatican Observatory all contribute to a unique perspective within the field. For amateur astronomers and Catholics alike, exploring these implications offers a rich and rewarding journey through the wonders of the universe.

Creation and the Big Bang Theory

The concept of creation and its relationship to the Big Bang Theory has been a subject of great interest and debate among both amateur astronomers and Catholics. In this subchapter, we will explore the pioneering contributions of the Vatican Observatory to astronomy and how they have shed light on the connection between creation and the Big Bang Theory.

The Vatican Observatory, established in 1891, has played a vital role in advancing our understanding of the universe and reconciling scientific discoveries with Catholic teachings. One of its most significant contributions has been in the field of cosmology, particularly the study of the origins of the universe.

The Big Bang Theory, proposed in the early 20th century by Father Lemaitre, suggests that the universe originated from a single, incredibly dense and hot point, expanding rapidly over time. This theory has been widely accepted by the scientific community, but it also raises questions about the role of a creator in the process.

The Vatican Observatory has been at the forefront of exploring these questions and has found that the Big Bang Theory does not contradict the belief in a creator. In fact, it provides compelling evidence for the existence of God. The precise conditions required for the universe to come into being, the fine-tuning of physical constants, and the intricate laws of nature all point towards an intelligent designer.

Furthermore, the Vatican Observatory has emphasized the importance of interpreting the creation accounts in the Bible as allegorical rather than literal. This allows for a harmonious integration of scientific discoveries and religious beliefs. By understanding creation as a dynamic process guided by a loving creator, Catholics can appreciate the wonders of the universe without compromising their faith.

The observatory's research has also highlighted the need for humility in the face of the vastness and complexity of the cosmos. It encourages Catholics to embrace scientific advancements as a means of deepening their understanding and appreciation of God's creation.

The Vatican Observatory's pioneering contributions to astronomy have played a crucial role in bridging the gap between the Big Bang Theory and the belief in a creator. By exploring the scientific evidence while remaining faithful to their religious teachings, amateur astronomers and Catholics alike can gain a deeper understanding of the mysteries of the universe and the role of a creator in its existence.

The Existence of Extraterrestrial Life

In the vast expanse of the universe, the question of whether we are alone has captivated the imaginations of astronomers and laypeople alike. Are we, as humans, the only intelligent beings in the cosmos, or is there other life out there? This subchapter delves into the tantalizing possibility of extraterrestrial life and explores the Catholic Church's stance on this intriguing subject.

The Vatican Observatory's pioneering contributions to astronomy have not been limited to the study of celestial bodies within our solar system. The quest to understand the existence of extraterrestrial life has been a focal point of the Observatory's research. For centuries, the Catholic Church has embraced an open-minded approach towards this question, recognizing that scientific exploration can coexist harmoniously with the teachings of faith.

The Catholic Church's stance on the existence of extraterrestrial life is not explicitly defined, as it is considered a scientific, rather than a theological, question. However, there have been various statements and discussions by prominent figures within the Church regarding this topic. From the discovery of exoplanets to the exploration of extremophiles on Earth, the Observatory's contributions shed light on the potential habitats and conditions that could sustain extraterrestrial lifeforms.

Catholics, in particular, will find solace in the Church's stance on this matter. The subchapter delves into the theological implications of extraterrestrial life, highlighting how the Catholic faith can accommodate the existence of beings originating from other planets. Rather than viewing the search for extraterrestrial life as a threat to religious beliefs, the Vatican Observatory acknowledges that such discoveries would only deepen our appreciation for the vastness and complexity of God's creation.

The subchapter also examines the ethical and moral questions that arise from the potential discovery of intelligent extraterrestrial life. How would contact with an alien civilization impact our understanding of humanity's place in the universe? How would it affect our religious beliefs and practices? These thought-provoking inquiries encourage readers to ponder the profound implications of encountering life beyond our own planet.

Overall, this subchapter provides a captivating exploration of the existence of extraterrestrial life. It invites amateur astronomers to marvel at the scientific advancements made by the Vatican Observatory while assuring Catholics that their faith can coexist harmoniously with the search for intelligent life in the universe. By examining the contributions of the Vatican Observatory to the study of extraterrestrial life, this book encourages readers to broaden their horizons and embrace the awe-inspiring possibilities that lie beyond our world.

The Vatican Observatory's Perspective on Astrobiology

Astrobiology, the study of life in the universe, has always fascinated humanity. Are we alone in the vast expanse of space, or could there be other forms of life out there? This question has intrigued astronomers and philosophers alike for centuries. In this subchapter, we will explore the Vatican Observatory's perspective on astrobiology and its pioneering contributions to this fascinating field.

The Vatican Observatory, established in 1891, has a long and rich history of studying the heavens. While its primary focus has been on traditional astronomical research, the observatory has also made significant contributions to the emerging field of astrobiology. Drawing on the expertise of its eminent astronomers, the Vatican Observatory has provided a unique and thought-provoking perspective on the possibility of extraterrestrial life.

From a Catholic standpoint, the question of life beyond Earth raises theological and philosophical considerations. The Vatican Observatory's approach to astrobiology is deeply rooted in the belief that science and faith can coexist harmoniously. It recognizes that the search for life in the universe is not only a scientific endeavor but also a spiritual and philosophical quest.

One of the key contributions of the Vatican Observatory to astrobiology is its emphasis on the ethical implications of discovering extraterrestrial life. The observatory has engaged in discussions and debates about how the existence of intelligent life elsewhere in the universe could impact our understanding of humanity and our place in the cosmos. These conversations have given rise to important questions about the nature of God's creation and the significance of human life.

Furthermore, the Vatican Observatory has actively supported scientific research aimed at detecting and studying exoplanets, planets outside our solar system, which could potentially harbor life. Its astronomers have contributed to the development of advanced telescopes and instruments, enabling the discovery and characterization of exoplanets with unprecedented precision. By studying these distant worlds, the observatory seeks to deepen our understanding of the conditions necessary for life to exist in the universe.

Jesuit Father Jose Funes, the former director of the Vatican Observatory, suggested that if aliens exist, they may be a different life form that does not need Christ's redemption. He referred to them as "extraterrestrial brothers" and stated that Christians should consider the possibility of their existence as part of God's creative freedom.

In a 2002 interview, Brother Guy Consolmagno, a planetary scientist at the Vatican Observatory, expressed that the discovery of extraterrestrial life would not be a threat to the Catholic faith. He even humorously remarked that he would be happy to baptize aliens if they wanted to, emphasizing that any entity, regardless of its physical form, has a soul.

In conclusion, the Vatican Observatory's perspective on astrobiology offers a unique blend of scientific exploration, theological reflection, and philosophical contemplation. By engaging in the study of life beyond Earth, the observatory contributes to the broader dialogue between science and religion, offering insights that resonate with both amateur astronomers and Catholics alike. Its pioneering contributions to astrobiology have not only advanced our knowledge of the universe but also deepened our appreciation for the mysteries of creation.

Contributions to the Dialogue between Science and Religion

In the fascinating realm where science and religion intersect, the Vatican Observatory has played a pivotal role in promoting a fruitful dialogue between these seemingly divergent disciplines. This subchapter explores the significant contributions made by the Vatican Observatory to the ongoing conversation between science and religion, with a specific focus on the field of astronomy.

For amateur astronomers, the Vatican Observatory's pioneering contributions have been instrumental in advancing our understanding of the cosmos. Established in 1891 by Pope Leo XIII, the observatory has consistently produced groundbreaking research, contributing to numerous astronomical discoveries. From the study of celestial bodies to the exploration of cosmic phenomena, the Vatican Observatory's work has captivated the minds of astronomers worldwide.

But what sets the Vatican Observatory apart is its unique position as an institution rooted in the Catholic Church. This connection provides an opportunity for Catholics to explore the wonders of the universe through the lens of their faith. By actively engaging with scientific inquiry and discovery, it demonstrates that science and religion can coexist harmoniously.

Through its research and publications, the Vatican Observatory has made significant contributions to cosmology, astrophysics, and planetary sciences. It has fostered collaborations with eminent scientists from various religious and non-religious backgrounds, exemplifying the Vatican's commitment to open dialogue and intellectual exchange. These collaborations have led to groundbreaking discoveries, such as the confirmation of the Big Bang theory, the study of exoplanets, and the exploration of the nature of dark matter and dark energy.

Moreover, the Vatican Observatory's commitment to education and outreach ensures that its contributions extend beyond the scientific community. By organizing conferences, workshops, and public lectures, it seeks to bridge the gap between science and faith, inviting astronomers, Catholics, and the wider public to explore the wonders of the cosmos together.

The Vatican Observatory's pioneering contributions to astronomy have not only advanced our understanding of the universe but also fostered a dialogue between science and religion. Its unique position within the Catholic Church has allowed for a fruitful exploration of the cosmos through the lens of faith. By actively engaging with the scientific community and promoting intellectual exchange, the Vatican Observatory has exemplified the harmony that can exist between science and religion. For amateur astronomers and Catholics alike, the observatory's work serves as a testament to the power of curiosity, exploration, and the pursuit of truth.

Collaborations with Theologians and Philosophers

One of the most intriguing aspects of the Vatican Observatory's contributions to astronomy is its unique collaborations with theologians and philosophers. The intersection of science, faith, and philosophy has long been a subject of interest for many, and the Vatican Observatory has played a vital role in fostering fruitful dialogues between these disciplines.

Throughout history, the Catholic Church has recognized the importance of reconciling scientific discoveries with theological and philosophical teachings. The Vatican Observatory, established in 1891, seeks to uphold this tradition by engaging in interdisciplinary collaborations that enrich our understanding of both the natural world and the spiritual realm.

By partnering with theologians, the Vatican Observatory aims to explore the profound questions that arise at the interface of science and religion. These collaborations have led to fascinating discussions on topics such as the origins of the universe, the nature of life on other planets, and the existence of extraterrestrial intelligent beings. Theologians bring a unique perspective to these inquiries, drawing from scripture, tradition, and theological principles to shed light on the implications of astronomical discoveries for our understanding of God's creation.

Similarly, collaborations with philosophers allow the Vatican Observatory to delve into the philosophical implications of astronomical research. Philosophers contribute by examining the underlying assumptions, logical implications, and ethical considerations of scientific theories. They help us reflect on the profound questions raised by astronomy, such as the nature of time, the existence of multiple universes, and the role of human beings within the vast cosmos.

By fostering collaborations with theologians and philosophers, the Vatican Observatory not only enriches the field of astronomy but also deepens our understanding of the Catholic faith. These interdisciplinary dialogues challenge scientists to consider the broader implications of their work and invite theologians and philosophers to engage with scientific discoveries in a meaningful way.

For amateur astronomers, these collaborations offer a unique opportunity to explore the connections between science and faith. They provide a window into the rich intellectual tradition of the Catholic Church and demonstrate the compatibility of scientific inquiry and religious belief. By examining the contributions of the Vatican Observatory to astronomy through the lens of theology and philosophy, readers can gain a more holistic understanding of the mysteries of the universe and their implications for human existence.

The collaborations between the Vatican Observatory, theologians, and philosophers have been instrumental in advancing our understanding of the universe and its connection to matters of faith and philosophy. By nurturing these interdisciplinary dialogues, the Vatican Observatory continues to make pioneering contributions to both the field of astronomy and the broader realms of theology and philosophy.

Engaging with the Scientific Community

In the vast world of astronomy, the Vatican Observatory has made significant contributions that have shaped our understanding of the universe. However, the efforts of this renowned institution would not have been possible without the engagement and collaboration of the scientific community. This subchapter explores the Vatican Observatory's approach to engaging with scientists and the wider astronomy community, highlighting the significance of their contributions and their unique perspective as Catholics.

The Vatican Observatory has always recognized the importance of fostering open dialogue and collaboration within the scientific community. By actively participating in conferences, workshops, and symposiums, the Vatican Observatory scientists have been able to present their research findings, exchange ideas, and engage in productive discussions with fellow astronomers. Their involvement in these events has facilitated the sharing of knowledge and the exploration of various astronomical topics.

Furthermore, the Vatican Observatory's engagement with the scientific community extends beyond conferences and workshops. The institution actively collaborates with other scientific organizations, universities, and research centers worldwide, fostering interdisciplinary research and encouraging the exchange of expertise. This collaboration has proven fruitful in expanding the scope of their research, as well as enriching the wider scientific community with their unique insights and contributions.

Engaging with the scientific community has also allowed the Vatican Observatory to bridge the gap between science and religion. As Catholics, the Observatory's scientists bring a distinct perspective to the field of astronomy. Their work demonstrates that science and faith can coexist harmoniously, challenging the notion that these realms are inherently at odds with each other. By engaging with the scientific community, the Vatican Observatory encourages a thoughtful dialogue on the intersection of science, faith, and our understanding of the universe.

For amateur astronomers and Catholics alike, the engagement of the Vatican Observatory with the scientific community offers an opportunity to delve deeper into the fascinating world of astronomy. The institution's contributions to the field have not only advanced our knowledge of the cosmos but have also enriched our understanding of the relationship between science and religion. By engaging with the scientific community, the Vatican Observatory continues to inspire and educate, making significant strides in the pursuit of knowledge and fostering a more comprehensive understanding of the universe.

In conclusion, the subchapter "Engaging with the Scientific Community" sheds light on the Vatican Observatory's active involvement with the scientific community and the impact of this engagement on the field of astronomy. By embracing collaboration, participating in conferences, and fostering interdisciplinary research, the Vatican Observatory has made valuable contributions and encouraged dialogue between science and faith. For amateur astronomers and Catholics, the engagement of the Vatican Observatory offers an enriching perspective on the wonders of the universe and the intersection of science and religion.

Promoting Interdisciplinary Research

In the pursuit of scientific knowledge, the importance of interdisciplinary research cannot be overstated. It is through the collaboration of experts from various fields that groundbreaking discoveries are made and new frontiers are explored. This subchapter delves into the Vatican Observatory's pioneering contributions in promoting interdisciplinary research, highlighting its impact on the realms of astronomy and Catholicism.

The Vatican Observatory, a renowned institution in the world of astronomy, has been at the forefront of fostering interdisciplinary research for centuries. By actively encouraging collaboration between astronomers, theologians, philosophers, and scientists from diverse backgrounds, the observatory has created a unique platform for the exchange of ideas, knowledge, and expertise.

One of the greatest benefits of interdisciplinary research is the ability to gain fresh perspectives and insights that may not be possible through a single disciplinary approach. The Vatican Observatory recognizes this and has actively sought to bridge the gap between science and religion, particularly within the Catholic faith. Through interdisciplinary research, astronomers have been able to explore the mysteries of the universe while respecting and integrating theological and philosophical perspectives.

The observatory's contributions to astronomy through interdisciplinary research are numerous and significant. By collaborating with experts in fields such as physics, mathematics, and astrophysics, the Vatican Observatory has made groundbreaking discoveries, expanded our understanding of the cosmos, and advanced scientific knowledge. Its interdisciplinary approach has facilitated the development of innovative research methodologies and tools, often leading to cutting-edge advancements in the field.

For Catholic amateur astronomers, the Vatican Observatory's commitment to interdisciplinary research is particularly appealing. By embracing multiple disciplines, the observatory provides a unique perspective that integrates scientific exploration with religious faith. This approach not only enriches our understanding of the universe but also fosters a sense of wonder and awe, aligning with the teachings and beliefs of the Catholic Church.

Promoting interdisciplinary research is a cornerstone of the Vatican Observatory's pioneering contributions to astronomy. By fostering collaboration between scientists, theologians, philosophers, and other experts, the observatory has paved the way for groundbreaking discoveries and advancements in the field. For amateur astronomers and Catholics alike, the interdisciplinary approach of the Vatican Observatory provides a fascinating and enriching perspective that combines scientific exploration with religious faith.

Chapter 5: The Future of Catholic Astronomy - The Vatican Observatory's Ongoing Work

"Charting the Celestial Horizon: The Vatican Observatory's Enduring Quest Towards Tomorrow's Cosmic Frontiers"

Current Research Projects and Initiatives

The Vatican Observatory has long been at the forefront of astronomical research, making significant contributions to our understanding of the cosmos. In this subchapter, we will explore some of the exciting current research projects and initiatives undertaken by the Vatican Observatory, highlighting its pioneering role in advancing the field of astronomy.

One of the major research projects currently underway at the Vatican Observatory is the study of exoplanets. With the discovery of thousands of exoplanets in recent years, astronomers are now focused on characterizing these distant worlds and determining their potential for hosting life. The Vatican Observatory is actively involved in observing and analyzing exoplanets, using advanced telescopes and instruments to gather data on their atmospheres, compositions, and orbits. By contributing to this cutting-edge research, the Vatican Observatory is playing a crucial role in expanding our knowledge of planetary systems beyond our own.

Another important area of research for the Vatican Observatory is the study of galactic evolution and formation. By observing and analyzing different galaxies, astronomers at the Vatican Observatory are unraveling the mysteries of how galaxies form, grow, and evolve over time. This research provides valuable insights into the origins and evolution of our own Milky Way galaxy, shedding light on the fundamental processes that have shaped the cosmos.

In addition to these specific research projects, the Vatican Observatory is also actively engaged in various initiatives aimed at promoting the dialogue between science and faith. Recognizing the compatibility between scientific inquiry and religious belief, the Vatican Observatory seeks to bridge the gap between these two domains, fostering a deeper understanding and appreciation for both. Through conferences, lectures, and publications, the Observatory encourages open discussions on the intersection of science, astronomy, and Catholicism, inviting astronomers and Catholics alike to explore the profound questions about the nature of the universe and our place within it.

For amateur astronomers and Catholics interested in the contributions of the Vatican Observatory to the field of astronomy, these ongoing research projects and initiatives offer a fascinating glimpse into the forefront of scientific exploration. By pushing the boundaries of knowledge and fostering dialogue between science and faith, the Vatican Observatory continues to make pioneering contributions that enrich our understanding of the universe and inspire us to contemplate the mysteries of creation.

Ongoing Observational Campaigns

In the realm of astronomy, the Vatican Observatory has made pioneering contributions, which continue to shape our understanding of the universe. One of the key aspects of their work involves ongoing observational campaigns that have significantly advanced our knowledge in various fields of astronomy.

These campaigns are a testament to the Vatican Observatory's commitment to conducting rigorous scientific research while upholding its Catholic values. By combining state-of-the-art technology with a deep appreciation for the wonders of creation, the observatory's ongoing observational campaigns have yielded groundbreaking discoveries and shed light on the mysteries of the cosmos.

One such campaign focuses on the study of exoplanets, planets that exist outside our solar system. Through advanced telescopes and sophisticated data analysis techniques, the observatory has been at the forefront of identifying and characterizing exoplanets, providing valuable insights into their formation, composition, and potential habitability. These efforts contribute to the broader understanding of the possibility of life beyond Earth, aligning with the Catholic belief in the existence of a Creator who imbues the universe with purpose.

Another ongoing observational campaign centers around the study of stellar evolution. By monitoring the life cycles of various stars, the Vatican Observatory has contributed to our understanding of stellar birth, death, and the processes that govern their evolution. This research has profound implications for our comprehension of the universe's origins and the natural laws that govern its functioning.

Additionally, the observatory's campaigns extend to the exploration of galaxies, the measurement of cosmic microwave background radiation, and the quest to understand the nature of dark matter and dark energy. These ongoing efforts exemplify the Vatican Observatory's dedication to pushing the boundaries of scientific knowledge and exploring the mysteries of the universe from a Catholic perspective.

For amateur astronomers, these ongoing observational campaigns offer a unique opportunity to delve into the latest research and discoveries in the field. By following the Vatican Observatory's work, enthusiasts can stay informed about the most recent advancements and gain a deeper appreciation for the beauty and complexity of the cosmos.

Catholics, too, can find inspiration in the Vatican Observatory's ongoing observational campaigns. These efforts showcase the harmonious relationship between faith and science, reinforcing the notion that exploring the wonders of the universe can be a spiritual endeavor. By studying the heavens, Catholics can gain a deeper understanding of God's creation and marvel at the intricate design that underlies the cosmos.

In summary, the Vatican Observatory's ongoing observational campaigns have played a pivotal role in advancing our knowledge of the universe. For amateur astronomers and Catholics alike, these campaigns offer a unique opportunity to explore the contributions of the Vatican Observatory to astronomy and gain a deeper appreciation for the wonders of creation.

Vatican Observatory's Role in Space Missions

The Vatican Observatory, founded in 1891, has played a significant role in advancing our understanding of the cosmos. While many may think of the

Vatican as solely a religious institution, it has made pioneering contributions to the field of astronomy over the years. This subchapter will delve into the observatory's involvement in space missions, showcasing the unique intersection of science and faith.

The Vatican Observatory has been actively engaged in studying celestial bodies, both from observatories on Earth and through collaborations with space agencies. One of its notable contributions to space missions was the Vatican Advanced Technology Telescope (VATT), located at the Mount Graham International Observatory in Arizona. The VATT, equipped with cutting-edge technology, has provided valuable insights into distant galaxies, black holes, and exoplanets. It has also supported NASA's missions by assisting in the discovery and characterization of exoplanets beyond our solar system.

Moreover, the Vatican Observatory has been involved in various space missions through collaborations with space agencies, including NASA and the European Space Agency (ESA). These collaborations have allowed the observatory's scientists to contribute their expertise in areas such as astrophysics, cosmology, and planetary science. For instance, the observatory's astronomers have played a crucial role in analyzing data from space telescopes like the Hubble Space Telescope and the Spitzer Space Telescope, enhancing our understanding of the universe's origins and evolution.

The Vatican Observatory's involvement in space missions is not limited to scientific contributions alone. It also serves as a bridge between science and faith, promoting dialogue and fostering understanding between the Catholic Church and the scientific community. By actively participating in space missions, the observatory demonstrates that scientific exploration and religious belief can coexist harmoniously.

For amateur astronomers, the Vatican Observatory's contributions to space missions offer a unique perspective on the wonders of the universe. The intersection of faith and science provides a rich tapestry of knowledge, nurturing a deeper appreciation for the cosmos and the mysteries it holds. Catholics, in particular, can take pride in the Vatican Observatory's ongoing efforts to reconcile scientific discoveries with their religious beliefs, inspiring a sense of awe and wonder at the grandeur of creation.

The Vatican Observatory's role in space missions is a testament to the institution's commitment to advancing scientific knowledge while promoting dialogue between science and faith. Its contributions to space missions through the VATT, collaborations with space agencies, and bridging the gap between science and religion make it a significant player in the field of astronomy. Whether you are an astronomy buff or a Catholic seeking to explore the intersections of science and faith, the Vatican Observatory's pioneering contributions to space missions are sure to captivate and inspire.

Exploring New Frontiers in Astronomy

In the vast expanse of the universe, humanity has always been captivated by the mysteries and wonders of the cosmos. From ancient civilizations to modern times, the study of astronomy has allowed us to unravel the secrets of the stars and understand our place in the universe. In this subchapter, we delve into the exciting realm of exploring new frontiers in astronomy, with a particular focus on the pioneering contributions of the Vatican Observatory.

Over the centuries, the Vatican Observatory has been at the forefront of astronomical research, making significant contributions to our understanding of the cosmos. This section explores some of the groundbreaking discoveries and advancements made by the observatory, while also shedding light on the intersection of Catholicism and astronomy.

One of the key areas in which the Vatican Observatory has made pioneering contributions is in the field of exoplanet research. This subchapter delves into the observatory's involvement in the discovery and study of planets beyond our solar system, highlighting their efforts in advancing our understanding of exoplanetary systems and the potential for extraterrestrial life.

Additionally, the Vatican Observatory has been instrumental in the study of stellar evolution and the life cycle of stars. Through their research, astronomers at the observatory have deepened our understanding of how stars are born, live, and die, shedding light on the fundamental processes that shape our universe.

Furthermore, this subchapter explores the vital role the Vatican Observatory plays in the field of astrophysics. From studying cosmic radiation to investigating the properties of dark matter and dark energy, the observatory's contributions to astrophysical research have been crucial in expanding our knowledge of the universe.

For amateur astronomers and Catholics alike, this subchapter serves as a testament to the Vatican Observatory's commitment to scientific inquiry and the pursuit of truth. It highlights the harmonious relationship between faith and science, demonstrating how the exploration of new frontiers in astronomy can deepen our appreciation for the wonders of creation.

In conclusion, "Exploring New Frontiers in Astronomy" is a captivating subchapter that showcases the pioneering contributions of the Vatican Observatory to the field of astronomy. It provides a glimpse into the groundbreaking discoveries made by the observatory, while also emphasizing the compatibility between faith and science. For astronomy enthusiasts and those interested in the unique intersection of Catholicism and astronomy, this subchapter offers an engaging and informative read.

The Vatican Observatory's Vision for the Future

As we delve into the captivating world of Catholic Astronomy and explore the contributions of the Vatican Observatory to this field, it is crucial to understand the vision that guides this esteemed institution into the future. The Vatican Observatory, with its rich history and pioneering contributions, has always strived to bridge the gap between science and faith. This subchapter delves into the Vatican Observatory's vision for the future, offering insight into its goals, aspirations, and the impact it aims to make on both the scientific and Catholic communities.

One of the primary facets of the Vatican Observatory's vision is to continue fostering the dialogue between science and religion. The institution firmly believes that science and faith are not mutually exclusive but rather complementary paths to understanding the world around us. By nurturing this dialogue, the Vatican Observatory hopes to dispel misconceptions and foster a more inclusive and harmonious relationship between these two realms.

Another crucial aspect of the Vatican Observatory's vision is the promotion of scientific literacy within the Catholic community. Recognizing the significance of a scientifically informed laity, the Observatory seeks to educate and engage Catholics about the wonders of the universe. By providing resources, organizing lectures, and hosting events, the Vatican Observatory aims to inspire curiosity and encourage a deeper appreciation of the beauty and complexity of God's creation.

In line with its commitment to scientific research, the Vatican Observatory envisions expanding its research capabilities and collaborations with leading scientific institutions worldwide. By investing in state-of-the-art equipment, technology, and talented astronomers, the Observatory aims to contribute even further to the field of astronomy. It seeks to push the boundaries of knowledge, unravel the mysteries of the cosmos, and shed light on the profound questions that have captivated humanity for centuries.

Furthermore, the Vatican Observatory's vision encompasses a commitment to environmental stewardship and the ethical implications of scientific advancements. Recognizing the importance of caring for the Earth, the institution seeks to promote dialogue and action on issues such as climate change, sustainable development, and responsible resource management. By integrating scientific knowledge with Catholic social teachings, the Vatican Observatory hopes to inspire individuals and communities to take an active role in preserving and protecting our planet.

Ultimately, the Vatican Observatory's vision for the future is rooted in a deep appreciation for the harmony between science and faith. By fostering dialogue, promoting scientific literacy, expanding research capabilities, and addressing environmental challenges, the Observatory aims to contribute to the betterment of society and the advancement of human knowledge. It is a vision that holds immense promise for both amateur astronomers and Catholics alike, offering a unique perspective that embraces the wonders of the universe and the profound mysteries of faith.

Expanding International Collaborations

One of the most remarkable aspects of the Vatican Observatory's pioneering contributions to astronomy is its commitment to expanding international collaborations. Over the years, this renowned institution has fostered partnerships and collaborations with scientists, researchers, and institutions from around the world, transcending geographical boundaries and religious affiliations. This subchapter explores the significance and impact of these international collaborations on the field of astronomy, appealing to amateur astronomers, Catholics, and those interested in the contributions of the Vatican Observatory.

From its inception, the Vatican Observatory recognized the importance of cooperation in advancing scientific knowledge. Recognizing that scientific progress knows no borders, the Vatican Observatory has actively sought out partnerships with leading institutions and scientists worldwide. By facilitating knowledge exchange, sharing resources, and promoting cultural and scientific exchanges, these collaborations have played a vital role in the Observatory's pioneering contributions to astronomy.

The Vatican Observatory's international collaborations have been instrumental in promoting interfaith dialogue and fostering cultural understanding. By engaging with diverse religious and cultural backgrounds, the Observatory has successfully bridged gaps and encouraged mutual respect among different communities. This unique approach has not only enriched the field of astronomy but has also contributed to broader efforts of promoting peace and harmony.

Through its collaborations, the Vatican Observatory has gained access to cutting-edge technology, observational facilities, and data from different parts of the world. This access has allowed its researchers to embark on groundbreaking studies and contribute to significant discoveries. The sharing of resources has also been mutually beneficial, as the Observatory has been able to offer its expertise and contribute to the scientific endeavors of its collaborators.

Furthermore, these collaborations have opened up opportunities for young astronomers and scientists to work with leading experts in the field. By providing a platform for international cooperation, the Vatican Observatory has nurtured talent and encouraged the next generation to pursue their passion for astronomy.

The Vatican Observatory's commitment to expanding international collaborations has been a cornerstone of its pioneering contributions to astronomy. By transcending geographical and religious boundaries, the Observatory has fostered knowledge exchange, promoted cultural understanding, and facilitated groundbreaking research. These collaborations have not only enriched the field of astronomy but have also served as a valuable tool for promoting interfaith dialogue and fostering peace. For amateur astronomers, Catholics, and those interested in the contributions of the Vatican Observatory, these international collaborations exemplify the Observatory's dedication to advancing scientific knowledge and promoting unity among different communities.

Developing New Observational Technologies

One of the key aspects of the Vatican Observatory's pioneering contributions to astronomy is its commitment to developing new observational technologies. Over the years, the Vatican Observatory has played a vital role in advancing the field of astronomy by pushing the boundaries of technology and innovation.

The quest to understand the mysteries of the universe has always driven astronomers to refine and improve their observational tools. From Galileo's first telescope to the state-of-the-art instruments used today, technological advancements have been instrumental in expanding our knowledge of the cosmos. The Vatican Observatory has been at the forefront of this technological revolution, continuously striving to develop cutting-edge instruments.

One of the significant achievements of the Vatican Observatory in terms of observational technologies is the creation of advanced telescopes. These telescopes, designed and built by the talented team of scientists and engineers at the Vatican Observatory, have revolutionized the way we observe celestial bodies. By incorporating the latest advancements in optics, detectors, and imaging techniques, these telescopes provide astronomers with unprecedented clarity and precision in their observations.

Furthermore, the Vatican Observatory has also made significant contributions to the field of radio astronomy. Radio telescopes, capable of detecting radio waves emitted by celestial objects, have opened up new avenues of exploration in astronomy. The Vatican Observatory has actively participated in the development of sensitive radio receivers and interferometers, allowing astronomers to study phenomena such as pulsars, quasars, and cosmic microwave background radiation.

In addition to telescopes, the Vatican Observatory has been actively involved in the development of space-based observatories. Collaborating with international partners, the Vatican Observatory has contributed to the design and construction of telescopes that orbit the Earth or are placed on satellites. These space-based observatories have the advantage of observing the universe free from the interference of Earth's atmosphere, providing unparalleled data for astronomers.

The Vatican Observatory's commitment to developing new observational technologies is rooted in its belief that understanding the natural world and the cosmos is essential to deepening our understanding of God's creation. By pushing the boundaries of technology and innovation, the Vatican Observatory's contributions have not only advanced the field of astronomy but also inspired countless individuals, both within the Catholic community and beyond, to marvel at the wonders of the universe.

The Vatican Observatory's pioneering contributions to astronomy extend beyond its research and observations. Its dedication to developing new observational technologies has propelled the field forward, enabling astronomers to explore the universe with unprecedented clarity and precision. By continuously pushing the boundaries of technology and innovation, the Vatican Observatory has not only expanded our knowledge of the cosmos but has also inspired generations of amateur astronomers and Catholics to explore the beauty and mysteries of the universe.

Addressing Contemporary Challenges in Astronomy

In the ever-evolving field of astronomy, scientists and researchers face numerous contemporary challenges that push the boundaries of our knowledge about the universe. From technological advancements to the exploration of new cosmic phenomena, these challenges require innovative approaches and collaboration among astronomers worldwide. In this subchapter, we will delve into some of the most pressing issues and how the Vatican Observatory has made pioneering contributions to address them.

One of the foremost challenges in modern astronomy is the exploration of dark matter and dark energy. These mysterious entities, which constitute the majority of the universe, have captivated scientists for decades. The Vatican Observatory has actively supported research in this area, employing sophisticated techniques and instruments to study their effects on celestial objects. By analyzing the behavior of galaxies and the cosmic microwave background radiation, the observatory has contributed to unraveling the secrets of dark matter and dark energy, shedding light on the nature of our universe.

Another contemporary challenge lies in the detection and study of exoplanets, planets that orbit stars outside our solar system. The discovery of these distant worlds has revolutionized our understanding of planetary systems and the potential for extraterrestrial life. The Vatican Observatory has been at the forefront of exoplanet research, collaborating with international teams to develop advanced telescopes and observation methods. By participating in projects like the Transiting Exoplanet Survey Satellite (TESS) and the European Southern Observatory's High Accuracy Radial velocity Planet Searcher (HARPS), the Vatican Observatory has made significant contributions to expanding our knowledge of exoplanets.

Furthermore, the observatory has addressed the challenges posed by the ever-increasing amount of astronomical data. With the advent of powerful telescopes and advanced data analysis techniques, astronomers are faced with an overwhelming volume of information. The Vatican Observatory has pioneered data management and analysis methods, contributing to the development of cutting-edge technologies for processing and interpreting astronomical data. By collaborating with other institutions and sharing their expertise, the observatory has played a vital role in ensuring the efficient utilization of the vast amount of data generated by modern observatories.

For amateur astronomers and Catholics interested in the Contributions of the Vatican Observatory to Astronomy, this subchapter offers a fascinating insight into the contemporary challenges faced by astronomers. It highlights the innovative approaches and pioneering contributions of the Vatican Observatory in addressing these challenges, furthering our understanding of the universe and our place within it. By exploring topics such as dark matter, exoplanets, and data management, this subchapter aims to inspire readers to appreciate the immense progress made by the Vatican Observatory and the ongoing endeavors to unlock the secrets of the cosmos.

Conclusion: The Enduring Legacy of the Vatican Observatory

"Unveiling the Celestial Tapestry: The Timeless Legacy of the Vatican Observatory's Cosmic Journey"

Throughout the centuries, the Vatican Observatory has made significant contributions to the field of astronomy, leaving an enduring legacy that continues to inspire both amateur astronomers and Catholics alike. This subchapter aims to summarize the key contributions of the Vatican Observatory and highlight its importance in the realm of scientific exploration.

The Vatican Observatory's journey began in 1582 when Pope Gregory XIII established the Gregorian calendar to rectify the discrepancies in the Julian calendar. This marked the Vatican's recognition of the importance of astronomy in understanding the workings of the universe. Since then, the Vatican Observatory has played a pivotal role in advancing our knowledge of the cosmos.

One of the most notable contributions of the Vatican Observatory is its commitment to scientific research. The observatory has consistently produced groundbreaking work, particularly in the fields of stellar spectroscopy, solar physics, and planetary science. Its state-of-the-art instruments and dedicated scientists have made significant discoveries, expanding our understanding of celestial bodies and their evolution.

Furthermore, the Vatican Observatory has fostered a harmonious relationship between science and faith. By promoting dialogue between astronomers and theologians, it has bridged the gap between these two seemingly disparate disciplines. This unique approach has allowed for a deeper understanding of the mysteries of the universe, while also emphasizing the compatibility of science and Catholicism.

The observatory's commitment to education and public outreach has also left an indelible mark. Its astronomers have not only contributed to scientific journals but have also authored numerous books and given lectures to share their knowledge with the wider public. By making astronomy accessible to all, the Vatican Observatory has inspired countless individuals, nurturing a sense of wonder and curiosity about the universe.

The Vatican Observatory has made pioneering contributions to the field of astronomy, leaving an enduring legacy that continues to shape our understanding of the cosmos. Its dedication to scientific research, promotion of dialogue between science and faith, and commitment to education have made it an invaluable institution in the realm of scientific exploration. Whether you are an astronomy buff, a Catholic, or simply fascinated by the wonders of the universe, the Vatican Observatory's legacy is one that continues to inspire and captivate.

Acknowledgments

In writing this book, "Catholic Astronomy: The Vatican Observatory's Pioneering Contributions," it is important to acknowledge the countless individuals and institutions who have contributed to the field of astronomy, particularly the Vatican Observatory. Their pioneering efforts and unwavering dedication have significantly advanced our understanding of the universe and bridged the realms of science and faith.

First and foremost, our heartfelt gratitude goes to the Vatican Observatory itself, an institution that has played a crucial role in promoting the dialogue between science and religion. The Vatican Observatory's commitment to scientific research and the pursuit of knowledge has been instrumental in shaping our understanding of the cosmos. Their tireless dedication to exploring the wonders of the Universe while upholding the teachings of the Catholic Church is truly remarkable.

We would like to express our deep appreciation to the talented astronomers and scientists who have worked at the Vatican Observatory over the years. Their groundbreaking research has made significant contributions to various fields of astronomy, including stellar evolution, planetary science, and cosmology. Their passion for discovery and their commitment to sharing knowledge have inspired generations of astronomers.

We are also grateful for the support and collaboration of fellow astronomers and research institutions worldwide. The Vatican Observatory's partnerships with renowned observatories and universities have fostered a spirit of cooperation and exchange of ideas, transcending geographical boundaries. Through these collaborations, groundbreaking discoveries have been made, pushing the boundaries of human knowledge.

To the Catholic Church, we extend our thanks for recognizing the importance of scientific exploration and for embracing the Vatican Observatory as an essential component of its mission. The Church's support has allowed the

Vatican Observatory to thrive and continue making pioneering contributions to the field of astronomy.

Lastly, we would like to express our gratitude to the readers of this book – the amateur astronomers and the Catholic community. Your curiosity, enthusiasm, and unwavering support have been the driving force behind our endeavor to shed light on the Vatican Observatory's remarkable contributions. We hope that this book will inspire and deepen your appreciation for the wonders of the universe, and the harmonious relationship between science and faith.

In conclusion, the acknowledgments section of this book serves as a testament to the collective efforts of countless individuals and institutions who have contributed to the field of astronomy, particularly the Vatican Observatory. Their dedication, collaboration, and unwavering commitment to both science and faith have forever shaped our understanding of the cosmos and paved the way for future astronomical discoveries.

Appendix: Glossary of Key Terms

In this appendix, we provide a comprehensive glossary of key terms related to the fascinating field of Catholic astronomy and the pioneering contributions of the Vatican Observatory to the study of celestial objects and phenomena. This glossary aims to assist amateur astronomers, Catholics, and those interested in the specific niche of the Vatican Observatory's contributions to better understand the concepts and terminology used throughout the book.

1. Vatican Observatory: The Vatican Observatory is an astronomical research institution based in Vatican City. Established in 1891, it has played a significant role in advancing our understanding of the universe and integrating science with the Catholic faith.

2. Astronomy: The scientific study of celestial objects, such as stars, planets, galaxies, and their interactions and behaviors.

3. Catholic Church: The largest Christian denomination, led by the Pope and guided by Catholic teachings and traditions.

4. Celestial Objects: Objects found in space, including stars, planets, moons, asteroids, comets, and galaxies.

5. Observational Astronomy: The branch of astronomy focused on observing and studying celestial objects directly through telescopes or other instruments.

6. Astrophysics: The branch of astronomy that applies the principles of physics to the study of celestial objects and phenomena, such as the behavior of stars, galaxies, and the structure of the universe.

7. Catholic Astronomer: A person who is both a practicing Catholic and an astronomer, seeking to integrate scientific knowledge with the teachings of the Catholic faith.

8. Stellar Evolution: The process through which stars change over time, from their formation to their eventual death or transformation.

9. Cosmology: The study of the origin, structure, and evolution of the universe as a whole.

10. Vatican Advanced Technology Telescope (VATT): A state-of-the-art telescope operated by the Vatican Observatory, located at the Mount Graham International Observatory in Arizona, USA.

11. Supernova: The explosive death of a massive star, resulting in a sudden increase in brightness that can outshine an entire galaxy.

12. Exoplanet: A planet that orbits a star outside our solar system.

This glossary provides just a glimpse into the extensive terminology and concepts covered in "Catholic Astronomy: The Vatican Observatory's Pioneering Contributions." By familiarizing themselves with these key terms, amateur astronomers and Catholics alike will gain a deeper understanding of the remarkable contributions the Vatican Observatory has made to the field of astronomy, bridging the gap between science and faith.

Bibliography

The field of astronomy has witnessed numerous groundbreaking discoveries and advancements throughout history. It is a field that has captivated the minds of both amateur astronomers and Catholics alike. In the book "Catholic Astronomy: The Vatican Observatory's Pioneering Contributions," readers are provided with an in-depth exploration of the remarkable contributions made by the Vatican Observatory to the field of astronomy.

To further enhance the understanding of these contributions, this subchapter presents a comprehensive bibliography that serves as a valuable resource for readers interested in delving deeper into the subject matter.

1. "The Heavens Proclaim: Astronomy and the Vatican" by Guy Consolmagno and Martha W. Schaefer (2011): This book offers a captivating glimpse into the history, mission, and scientific achievements of the Vatican Observatory. It provides an excellent foundation for understanding the significance of the observatory's contributions to astronomy.

2. "Brother Astronomer: Adventures of a Vatican Scientist" by Guy Consolmagno (2000): In this engaging memoir, Brother Guy Consolmagno, a Jesuit astronomer and director of the Vatican Observatory, shares his personal experiences and reflections on the intersection of faith and science. Readers will gain valuable insights into the inner workings of the Vatican Observatory and its pioneering research.

3. "The Galileo Affair: A Documentary History" edited by Maurice A. Finocchiaro (1989): This compilation of primary sources provides an in-depth examination of the infamous Galileo affair. It sheds light on the complex relationship between the Catholic Church and scientific advancements during the Renaissance period, offering a historical context for the Vatican Observatory's subsequent contributions.

4. "The Vatican Observatory: In the Service of Nine Popes" by Sabino Maffeo (2001): This authoritative work explores the history of the Vatican Observatory from its inception in 1891 to the present day. It provides a

comprehensive overview of the observatory's significant contributions to astronomical research and its evolving role within the Catholic Church.

5. "Catholicism and Science" by Peter M.J. Hess and Paul Allen (2011): This book examines the relationship between Catholicism and science, including the Vatican's approach to scientific inquiry. It offers a broader perspective on the Catholic Church's engagement with scientific advancements and the role of the Vatican Observatory in promoting scientific exploration.

These selected works serve as a starting point for readers interested in further exploring the contributions of the Vatican Observatory to astronomy. By delving into these resources, amateur astronomers and Catholics can gain a deeper appreciation for the Vatican Observatory's pioneering research and its invaluable role in advancing our understanding of the cosmos.

Don't miss out!

Click the button below and you can sign up to receive emails whenever Larry Culver publishes a new book. There's no charge and no obligation.

[1]

https://books2read.com/r/B-A-BEPDB-EBIWC

BOOKS 2 READ

Connecting independent readers to independent writers.

Don't miss out!

Visit the website below and you can sign up to receive emails whenever Larry Culver publishes a new book. There's no charge and no obligation.

https://books2read.com/r/B-A-BEPDB-ZOYWC

BOOKS 2 READ

Connecting independent readers to independent writers.